THE ART AND PRACTICE OF

BIVOCATIONAL MINISTRY

A PASTOR'S GUIDE

THE ART AND PRACTICE OF
BIVOCATIONAL MINISTRY

A PASTOR'S GUIDE

DENNIS BICKERS

BEACON HILL PRESS
OF KANSAS CITY

ISBN 978-0-8341-3095-1

Printed in the
United States of America

Cover Design: J.R. Caines
Interior Design: Sharon Page

10 9 8 7 6 5 4 3 2 1

DEDICATION

My heroes in the church world are those men and women who faithfully serve in bivocational ministry roles. For a long time your contributions and needs were sometimes ignored, and you may have felt that no one understood you or your passion for what you did. Even worse, you may have felt that no one appreciated your efforts. However, I want you to know that you are understood and appreciated. God, who called you to this ministry, both understands and appreciates all you do, and always has. Many in the church you serve also recognize the important ministry you provide, and even if they don't voice it as much as we might like, they appreciate you and what you mean to them and to the church.

I want you to know that I also understand and appreciate all you do to live out your calling. I understand the sacrifices you make and the way you try to balance all the demands that are made on your time. I know the price you pay as a bivocational minister. That is why I continually seek new ways to encourage you and invest in your lives. I also know the price your families pay as they share you with the church you serve.

You and your families are making a difference in the kingdom of God. The work you do is vitally important to the people you serve, and you should feel a holy pride that God has entrusted that work to you. Not everyone could do what you do, and that is why God has chosen *you* for this work. He knows you can. It's not always easy, and there are times when it can feel very lonely, but always remember you are not alone. God is with you, as are those who believe in you and in your work.

It is my prayer that you find this book to be a helpful resource as you face some of the challenges addressed within its pages. It is to you, my bivocational brother and sister friends, that I dedicate this book.

ACKNOWLEDGMENTS

Quite a few people made this book possible. It comes out of my thesis for my doctorate of ministry, so I need to thank my professors at Liberty Theological Seminary who made that program such an enjoyment. I especially want to thank the director of the DMin program when I enrolled, Dr. Frank Schmitt, for allowing me to participate in the program, and Dr. Ron Hawkins, who approved my thesis project and served as the chair. When I asked Dr. Hawkins why he was interested in serving as the chair of my thesis, he said he was interested in both bivocational ministry and coaching, and I knew he would be an excellent chair. Dr. Larry Mason was the reader for my thesis. Each of these individuals made my thesis project and dissertation better. I also have to thank the five bivocational pastors who were willing to be coached as part of the project and to write a brief paper on the experience.

Once again, Beacon Hill Press of Kansas City has been a great encouragement throughout the creation of this book. Bonnie Perry expressed an interest in it even before my last book was released. My editor, Audra Marvin, has again challenged me with her insights and questions that helped make this book a more valuable resource. Danielle Broadbooks has done a great job of coordinating this project and worked hard to keep me on the various deadlines required. I have been blessed to work with such a great group of people.

I have to thank my wife again for allowing me the time to write. When I think about spending the last thirty years in the ministry, I have to remember that she has also spent thirty years in ministry. Studying, ministering, and writing all require time, and she has consistently encouraged me to pursue the call God has on my life. I could have done none of those things without that support. Thanks, Faye. I love you.

CONTENTS

INTRODUCTION

In 1981 I became the bivocational pastor of Hebron Baptist Church near Madison, Indiana. I served in that capacity for twenty years before accepting a position with the American Baptist Churches of Indiana and Kentucky. In this new role, I was responsible for working with approximately eighty churches, half of which were led by bivocational pastors. I also had an additional portfolio responsibility of addressing the needs of all the pastors of bivocational churches in our region. All three decades of my ministry, I have focused on bivocational ministers and the churches they serve.

It was no surprise when I chose, as my sabbatical project in 2008, to look into what was happening with bivocational ministry in other denominations. During that project, I spoke with leaders from the American Baptist Churches, USA; the Southern Baptist Convention; the United Methodist Church; the Episcopal Church; the Presbyterian Church of the USA; the Mennonite Church; the Evangelical Lutheran Churches of America; and the Church of the Nazarene. I asked each of these leaders the same simple questions.

- What is happening with bivocational ministry in your denomination?
- What do you see happening with bivocational ministry in the future?
- What are you doing to intentionally seek persons God might be calling to this ministry?

- How do you address the training and developmental needs these ministers may have?

The answers were the same across denominational lines. Their numbers of bivocational ministers were increasing, although none could tell with any precision just how many bivocational ministers currently served in their denominations. The data collection systems they use simply don't provide exact numbers for bivocational ministers. All the leaders indicated a belief that the numbers of bivocational ministers will increase in the future. None of them had any official way to identify persons called to this ministry. As the United Methodist leader told me, "They find us more often than we find them." Finally, although each denomination had various training opportunities available, the opportunities varied widely throughout their respective judicatories, and only the United Methodists and the Evangelical Lutheran Churches of America *required* training before one could begin serving as a bivocational minister.

From my experience serving as a bivocational minister, leading workshops for bivocational ministers, and working with dozens of them, I am convinced that these individuals have needs that differ from those of their fully funded counterparts. While they do share some common needs and challenges, the mere fact of being bivocational brings with it some unique challenges and needs, and denominational leaders need to be more intentional in working with these bivocational ministers.

This led to my decision in 2009 to do my doctor of ministry project on coaching bivocational ministers for greater ministry effectiveness. My thesis was that coaching could be a useful tool for denominational leaders to use with their bivocational ministers. As a coach, one does not need to be an expert on bivocational ministry to be able to serve those ministering in that capacity. After getting approval for my thesis, I offered via my blog and a monthly e-newsletter to personally coach five bivocational ministers. Within a few days, I had received dozens of requests from bivocational ministers to receive coaching, of whom I chose five, one in Canada, and the other four in various locations in the United States. All were male because none of the few women who expressed interest had any current or active involvement in church ministries. The plan was for each individual to have six coaching sessions to address whatever issues they wanted. At the conclusion, they submitted a written report of the experience. This book comes out of that experience.

Defining Terms

Some terms I'll use throughout the book should be defined. The first is *bivocational pastor*, which I define as a minister who serves in a paid ministry position and has income from another source. That other source may be a full-time job, a part-time job, or even a pension. It does not include income from a working spouse, nor does it include pastors who serve more than one church and receive salary from each one. It is not unusual for bivocational ministers to receive larger salaries from their second jobs than they do from their churches. Often, the second job will not be ministry related.

This definition does have some drawbacks. There are well-known ministers who pastor churches that have an average attendance in the thousands every week who have become wealthy from popular books they have written. (This author is not one of them!) Their income from their book sales and the conferences they lead may well surpass their church incomes. In some cases, they even refuse salary from their churches due to their successful writing and speaking careers. Such persons could not be considered bivocational, even though they have outside income apart from their church salary.

Normally, we find bivocational ministers serving in smaller churches, but there are exceptions. In previous books I have written about a friend of mine who served as a bivocational pastor to a church of 600 people. He and all his staff were bivocational by choice because they believed that was the best way to serve a church. While there are others serving larger congregations as bivocational pastors, they are the exception. Most bivocational pastors serve smaller churches.

The second term that needs defining is *fully funded*. I use this term in place of *full time*. If we have full-time pastors, then it logically follows that we have part-time pastors, but I don't know any part-time pastors. Although *part time* is often used to describe bivocational ministers, I find it demeaning to the ministers (which, to my knowledge, is *all* ministers) who are on call 24/7/365. As I often say in my workshops, when I looked at my calendar, I had fifty-two Sundays, just like every other pastor. Sermons had to be prepared, and I didn't have staff to preach on some of those Sundays. I had people who were admitted to the hospital and wanted to be visited by the pastor. I had people who wanted to be married, and I had funerals to preach. I was a full-time bivocational minister.

A *fully-funded* pastor, on the other hand, is one who receives all of his or her income from the church being served. Many fully-funded ministers receive small honorariums for weddings, funerals, preaching revivals, and other services they provide, but these are normally an insignificant percentage of their income and do not make them bivocational.

The third term is *coaching*. My favorite definition of coaching comes from Gary Collins, who writes that "coaching is the art and practice of guiding a person or group from where they are toward the greater competence and fulfillment that they desire."[1]

Finally, another term that may not be familiar to some readers is *judicatory leader*. In some denominations, these persons would be called district superintendents. They may be called area ministers or directors of missions in other denominations. They are people who provide resources, oversight, and leadership to their districts or state conventions.

Target Audience

There are several people who will benefit from reading this book. One group is denominational leaders who work with bivocational ministers. For some of you, bivocational ministry may be foreign to your understanding of traditional ministry. Your training and experience have been with fully-funded pastors, and you are most comfortable working with those churches and leaders. You may not even know for sure how to assist the bivocational ministers for whom you assume responsibility. One of the reasons I was selected for my current judicatory role was my experience as a bivocational minister. Everyone else on our region staff had experience in larger churches before beginning regional ministry. Our executive minister realized that the numbers of bivocational ministers were increasing in our region and wanted someone on staff who had experience in that work. Since then, I've been invited to address members of various judicatories, specifically to help them understand bivocational ministry and how they can best assist the people in their judicatories who serve in that capacity. If you find yourself uncertain how to minister to your bivocational leaders, you will find this book helpful.

A second group who can benefit from this book is the members of bivocationally pastored churches. It will be helpful for you to understand some of the challenges your pastor faces, and ways that other pastors and churches have worked together to resolve those same challenges. It is becoming increasingly important to keep the pastors you have as long as possible, assuming they provide effective ministry. Providing small salary and benefit increases as well as additional time off will be less costly to the church than being without a pastor while searching for a new one. Helping bivocational pastors address the challenges they face at work, at the church, and in the home will reap even greater appreciation and loyalty from the pastors.

The third and largest group of persons who will benefit from this book will be bivocational ministers themselves. I will share some of the questions and challenges the ministers I coached brought to our sessions and how we addressed them. In addition to the five I specifically coached for my DMin project, I have coached several other bivocational ministers and will include discussion of some of their issues as well. Some of these issues will be similar to ones you currently face, and the answers we found for them might be helpful to you. It is my prayer that you will be able to coach yourself through some of the challenges you face as you read stories similar to your own.

THE CONCEPTS

The chapters in this section will examine the broader concepts of bivocational ministry and coaching in order to foster a better understanding of bivocational ministers and some of the unique challenges they face. A deeper understanding of bivocational ministers could do much to dispel the misconceptions many people—including other ministers—have about the work they do. One of the goals of my ministry is to raise the level of appreciation for bivocational ministry. No one should consider bivocational ministry a lesser form of ministry. It is a legitimate call of God on a person's life that meets a growing need in the kingdom of God. The people who answer that call are special people who deserve to be respected and equipped with the tools they need to do their job.

We will also explore an overview of coaching that will help us better understand the benefits coaching can provide. I have found coaching to be an effective way to work with all ministers but particularly bivocational ministers. We will look at some of the personal qualities found in good coaches, how people know they are ready to be coached, and some things to be considered when selecting a coach. Self-coaching is also an option, and we will explore that possibility as well, and how you can use regular coaching skills to coach yourself.

.

CHAPTER ONE

UNDERSTANDING BIVOCATIONAL MINISTRY

Many trace bivocational ministry back to the apostle Paul, who supported himself and his ministry as a tentmaker. For many churches, having a bivocational minister was the norm until the 1950s, when denominations began to challenge their churches to support fully-funded pastors. In the United States, bivocational ministers served churches as the people moved west, supporting themselves as farmers, store owners, schoolteachers, and many other occupations while also providing pastoral care to their congregations and leading worship on Sunday mornings.

Starting in the 1950s, more denominations began to move toward professional ministry. Seminary education became more important as some denominations began to require the master of divinity for ordination, which further reduced the numbers of bivocational ministers. Education and ordination became wedges that divided bivocational ministers from their fully-funded counterparts. Many fully-funded ministers and denominational leaders looked down on bivocational ministers and viewed them as something less than real ministers.

As churches began, collectively, to move away from bivocational ministers, denominations and seminaries did little to promote the option. As a Bible school student in the early 1980s, I remember two individuals from the denomination coming into one of our classes and asking if any of us would be interested in helping start some new churches in a large city in another state. I asked if they would be using bivocational persons for that work. One of them quickly replied that new-church planting required more work than a bivocational person could provide. I still remember the disgusted tone in his voice as he dismissed the possibility that bivocational ministers could plant churches. Of course, today, bivocational persons are very involved in new-church planting, and it has proven to be a very effective way to start a new church.

Despite being told by various denominational leaders that their numbers of bivocational ministers were growing and are expected to keep growing, I could find no denomination with a staff person specifically assigned to work with bivocational ministers and their churches. For many years, the Southern Baptist Convention had a bivocational ministry consultant until Leon Wilson retired in 2003, at which time the position was eliminated. Despite the fact that this denomination expects their bivocational ministers to soon surpass the number of fully-funded pastors, they continue to neglect to fill that position.[1] Some mid-level judicatories do have persons assigned to work with bivocational ministers in their districts, but I can't find any denomination with an individual solely assigned to that responsibility.

This lack of support is also seen in the absence of resources that have been developed especially for bivocational ministers. Walk into any Christian bookstore and you can find numerous resources for mid-size and larger churches, but there are few resources for bivocational ministers and their churches.

The resource problem isn't limited to written resources. There are few workshops offered that pertain primarily to bivocational ministers, although that is beginning to change. In recent years I have been privileged to lead workshops for bivocational and small-church ministers for several different denominational organizations. One workshop I led in Canada demonstrated how hungry these small-church leaders are for training when one participant told me he drove nine hours one way to attend.

Many denominations offer regular pastors' gatherings to encourage peer support and fellowship and to provide training and promotion of the denomination's activities. However, many of these are held during the week while bivocational ministers often have to be at their other jobs. This leads to many bivocational ministers feeling like second-class citizens in their own denominations.

It's no wonder so many of them feel isolated and alone. Many bivocational ministers feel a great deal of stress due to the constant demands on their time and energy, and this sense of isolation and the lack of respect they feel from their denominations just add to that stress. We should not be surprised that burnout and depression are known among bivocational ministers. Archibald Hart explains why:

> The loneliness of ministry, although essentially positive, can shape the minister toward being cut off from support systems. It can keep him from having close confidants with whom problems of the work can be discussed. It is a psychological fact that one cannot resolve conflicts or clarify issues simply by thinking about them. Self-talk and introspective rumination with no outside input lead inevitably to distortion and irrationality, whereas talking things over with someone else can help clarify issues and remove distortions. Every minister needs close confidants—staff, family, other ministers, trusted laypersons in the congregation—

to help in this clarifying process. If steps are not deliberately taken to develop these trusting and supportive relationships in each pastorate, the loneliness of leadership responsibility will lead to isolation and a distortion of reasoning—and this spells depression for many ministers.[2]

Unfortunately, my own experience confirms Hart's words. I've written elsewhere about the clinical depression I experienced early in my pastorate. There is no question that a sense of isolation was a contributing factor to that depression. I did not feel that I had anyone to turn to as the stress levels began to increase. When the depression finally overwhelmed me, it took a year of medication and counseling to get well. Perhaps it could have been avoided if I'd had someone to talk to when the pressures began to intensify.

Ministry Challenges in the 21st Century

Bivocational ministers have the same responsibilities as fully-funded ministers. There are sermons to prepare each week, people who seek counsel, conflicts that arise in the church, administrative tasks, meetings to coordinate and attend, congregants who need to be visited, and the various other general expectations people have of ministers, regardless of church size.

There are also challenges associated with living in the 21st century. It's not easy to be a minister today. The way people think and believe is rapidly changing. Expectations are higher today than ever before, and if people can't get their expectations met, they will simply move on to another church. Denominational affiliation matters little in the 21st century. If people have to attend two or three different churches to have their expectations met, they will do so. In the past, it was enough for ministers to be able to exegete the Scriptures in order to preach to people. Today it is just as important to exegete the culture to understand how best to reach it, but when we do so, we begin to see just how difficult it is to minister to this postmodern, pre-Christian society in which we live.

Rejection of Absolute Truth

We are trying to preach a message of truth to a generation that has rejected absolute truth. While postmodern people are willing to accept that you may believe something to be true, they will not accept that you have the right to proclaim that the belief is true for all people. It seems that the only absolute truth that is acceptable today is that there is no such thing as absolute truth.

Once absolute truth is rejected, it follows that moral absolutes will also be rejected. Persons holding to such views do not accept someone stating that the moral choices people make are wrong, and they reject anyone who claims that some moral choices are superior to others. An obvious example of this today is the debate over same-sex marriage. The person who claims that homosexuality is a sin is immediately branded homophobic and unloving. There is great pressure today for the church to accept the mindset that all moral choices are valid, and the church itself has divided. A number of mainline denominations now ordain homosexuals to the ministry while others debate it (sometimes heatedly) at their national gatherings. Ministers who attempt to address the issue from a biblical perspective are under great pressure.

The pressure intensifies when a homosexual couple begins to attend a church. How does the church address this issue in a way that is consistent with the Bible's teaching yet also in a way that honors all mankind as persons of worth and value due to their being created in the image of God? A similar problem arises when an unmarried couple who live together want to join a church.

Without a belief in absolute truth and morals, it's virtually impossible to say anything is wrong. Everyone is free to make whatever choices they want to make, but this can only lead to chaos and eventual hurt for everyone. The problem becomes even worse when it begins to involve people from within the church family. Christians who loudly attack homosexuality may change their beliefs if their own children suddenly announce they are homosexual. A Christian husband finds himself in a relationship with another woman and divorces his wife to marry the new woman, and he cannot understand why the church wants to remove him from his leadership positions.

It's easy to believe in moral absolutes—until those absolutes personally impact our choices or those of family members; then, issues that were once black and white become various shades of gray. Churches look to their ministers for leadership as they wrestle with social issues, and pastors can quickly get caught in the middle. To take a stand and say that some choices are wrong because they violate clear, biblical teaching will get many pastors in trouble in today's climate of moral relativism.

Generational Differences

Many churches have four or even five generations of people attending services, and it's not easy to develop services and ministries that meet the needs of each generation. This complication is especially noticeable in the smaller churches in which many bivocational ministers serve, and is one reason so many churches struggle with worship wars. How many people enjoy the same music their grandparents enjoyed? Some churches offer blended services that try to provide both traditional and contemporary music, but such attempts are not always successful.

The challenge to church leaders is to provide environments for each generation to worship in meaningful ways. Go into any music store and watch how many people buy music for the pipe organ. You probably won't see many. Churches that only offer that type of worship experience are unlikely to attract a lot of younger people, but on the other hand, it is wrong to discard the traditional worship service in favor of the young, thereby denying a meaningful worship experience to older generations. This is not an easy problem to resolve.

Generational differences are not limited to music preferences. Younger generations are more visual than older generations, which is why many churches have added video-projection systems to their sanctuaries. Unfortunately, this too is not always well received, especially if it conflicts with one of the sacred cows of the church.

One church added a video system, but the older members complained that the screen, for which they paid a good sum of money, blocked the view of the cross behind the pulpit. They wanted to be able to see the cross. The church leaders compromised by raising the screen during the message. People agreed to the compromise, but some from both camps were frustrated by the decision. The pastor cannot use the video system during his actual message, so the church basically paid for a very expensive method to convey announcements. And by the way, many of those announcements are still read from the pulpit at the start of the service because older members insist they won't know what is happening in the church if the announcements are not read. The pastor of this particular church tells me this is an ongoing source of tension.

Membership Issues

Many people today are reluctant to commit to joining any organization, yet many churches require people to be members before they can participate in ministry or leadership roles. Although people don't want to join a church, they do want to be involved in things that are meaningful to them. How can churches utilize the gifts and passions these people bring when they are hesitant to join the church?

I recently had a call from a pastor who told me an individual had been attending his church for a few months and had expressed interest in becoming a member. The church was a Baptist church, and the prospective individual had a Methodist background. A problem arose because this particular Baptist church had a requirement in its constitution that all members of the church be baptized by immersion, a condition the individual was not willing to meet. He had previously been baptized in the Methodist tradition by sprinkling, and it was a meaningful event in his life. This man felt that being baptized again would lessen the significance of his original experience. The pastor asked me how he could address the problem.

I contacted a number of Baptist pastors and found they have been running into the same issue. Some took a traditional Baptist stance and said that anyone who wanted to be a member of their church would have to be immersed. Others said they did not believe differences in the baptism method should be a consideration for church membership. They were more interested in the individual's personal relationship with Jesus Christ than they were with the way the person had been baptized. A couple of pastors said their constitution required anyone who had not been baptized to be baptized by immersion but that, if someone had previously been baptized, it would be accepted regardless of the method.

As the denominational labels on our churches become less important to persons seeking a church to attend, I expect we will encounter this issue more often, and it is important that churches begin to address some decisions before being confronted with them. Lead pastors will be expected to facilitate those discussions, and they could be difficult in some churches.

Rapid Cultural Changes

The world is changing at a speed never before seen, and most churches struggle to keep up, if they even try. The smaller churches most often served by bivocational ministers are quite fond of life as it was in the 1950s, and some haven't decided yet whether to enter the twenty-first century. Although these churches may hold the pastor accountable for reaching our postmodern generation, they tend to resist nearly every change that will be required *to* reach that generation, and then they blame the pastor for not growing the church. As one might imagine, such attitudes place a tremendous strain on pastors.

The number of single-parent homes continues to increase, putting additional pressures on our society and the family, and this pressure invariably finds its way into the church. Virtually every study done on single-parent homes finds that there is a greater likelihood of economic difficulty; lower grades and increased social challenges for children; physical and mental exhaustion for the single parent; and increased chances of drug and/or alcohol abuse. This isn't to say that *every* single-parent home will have these issues, but studies consistently find that such issues are more often found in these homes.

Churches must revisit their children's ministry philosophies to ensure that children from single-parent homes receive the support and ministry they need. This can be a challenge in larger churches, with staff who are specifically hired to focus on children's ministries; it becomes much tougher for a smaller church, with a single minister on staff, working with lay volunteers. It is also likely that the church will only see these children every two weeks because they may be with the other parent the other week.

It is equally important not to forget the needs of the single parent. Does the Young Married Sunday school class really have much to say to a single parent, or does the name itself send a message that the church is focused on married couples to the exclusion of never-married or divorced persons? Even if that is not the *name* of the class, if everyone else in the class is married, the unmarried person may well feel like a fifth wheel, and neglect to participate. The bivocational pastor often struggles trying to find a way to minister both to married couples and single parents in a manner that will be meaningful to each one.

Of course, it can get even more difficult when trying to minister to young people. Again looking at a Young Married class, how will it minister to the needs of the twenty-nine-year-old grandmother? Such scenarios are part of our culture today, and sometimes they find their ways into our churches, praying to find *something* that will inspire hope and encouragement. I do not personally know of a bivocational church that could do that with the current ministries they have to offer.

Young families are the group that many smaller churches want to target. As I have met with pastor search committees in bivocational churches and asked what they were looking for in their next pastor, almost every one of them said the church needed a pastor who could grow their youth group and reach young families. They see youth and young families as their only hope of survival. However, most of them do not know what they are asking for. They do not understand the societal changes that impact the lives of young people and young families. To effectively reach these two groups would require a major shift of ministry priorities for most churches, and few of them would accept such changes.

I recently met with such a church. True to form, when I asked what they needed in their next pastor, they responded that he or she should be able to grow the church. Specifically, they wanted to see the pastor reach out to youth and young families. I then referred them to a survey I had asked them to have the congregation complete before I met with them. Of the top eight ministry specialties the congregation said they wanted in their new pastor, seven of them were inward focused. I pointed out this discrepancy to the committee: They were telling me the church needed a pastor who could grow the church, but the congregation said they wanted a chaplain who would care for their needs. I explained that any pastor who came into a role at that church thinking he or she had a mandate to grow the church would soon run into problems because of unmet expectations the congregation would have. Unfortunately, this is not an uncommon problem in many churches, and it has shortened the tenure of many good pastors.

Because of the changes taking place throughout society, ministers need to reinvent themselves fairly often. Futurist Leonard Sweet writes:

> No matter what your profession or company, you will need to re-invent yourself at least every seven years... If seminary education is ever to be seen as a system of lifelong learning, not a three-year event, it must break out of the classroom walls and get into the churches and communities where ministry takes place.[3]

Looking back at my twenty-year pastorate at Hebron Baptist Church, I can recognize a number of changes in my ministry style over that period of time. Some of it was because I learned new skills as I pursued an education, but some of it was a result of societal changes that required new approaches toward leadership. I completely changed my preaching style three times. I changed the way I led meetings, the way I dealt with conflict, how I dealt with difficult people, and the way I did outreach. During that time, I went from being a pastor who felt burdened to do the work of the church to one who recognized it as my responsibility to equip others to do ministry.

The problem with making changes in the way ministers approach their work is that there will inevitably be people who prefer the old way. A church that wants a chaplain isn't going to be happy with an equipping pastor. Churches that thrive on traditional forms of worship are not going to be happy when the pastors suggest that more contemporary forms of worship might better reach the people the churches claims they wants to reach. Churches that expect their pastors to wear suits and ties may not react well when they step into the pulpit wearing khakis and a polo shirt, even if they explain that formal attire can be a turn-off to some people.

A church that expects its pastor to stand directly behind the pulpit when preaching and always use the King James Version may express displeasure when their pastor does neither. I have been a visiting preacher in a few churches and been criticized after the service because I walk around when I preach. People said it was too distracting. In one church I visited, I was criticized because I used the New King James Version rather than the original KJV. That church's constitution actually required that only the King James Version could be used from the pulpit. (I never returned to that church to preach.)

Unique Challenges of the Bivocational Minister

An entire book could be written on the pressures ministers face due to the changes occurring in our society today, but even those few illustrate the tremendous challenges clergy members encounter. Additionally, bivocational ministers have some unique challenges that fully-funded ministers do not.

Time Constraints

Most ministers wish they had more time to do all the things they need to do, but, due to their other source(s) of employment, bivocational ministers experience obvious time constraints that fully-funded ministers do not. Virtually every bivocational minister I have coached or talked to in a workshop setting has said that time is the number-one challenge in his or her life. A minister who works a forty-hour week—as I did during much of my pastoral ministry—does not have those forty hours available for ministry purposes. That means everything else—whether personal or ministerial—must be condensed into the remaining hours, adding enormous pressure to the minsters and their families.

Bivocational ministers often feel they lack adequate time to prepare their sermons. They frequently go to bed at night knowing there is unfinished work they simply did not have time to do. This can generate feelings that they are not doing the work God has called them to do and cause them to doubt God's call on their lives.

In recent months I have read some blogs that discuss bivocational ministry. Many of the writers question whether bivocational ministry could even be a viable option. They do not believe bivocational ministers are able to give the time to the ministry that is required. Unfortunately, too many bivocational ministers struggle with the same thoughts and often condemn themselves for not having more time to give to the church.

The challenge is to find balance between the things that must happen to maintain one's well-being and the obligatory tasks one must accomplish. In my first book, *The Tentmaking Pastor*, I discussed five primary areas of one's life that must be kept in balance: God, family, ministry responsibilities, second job, and self-care.[4] Since that book is now out of print, let's take a brief look at each of these.

God. I found out while attending Bible college and during my pastoral ministry how easy it is to neglect one's personal relationship with God while involved in ministry. We can easily slip into the mindset that doing God's work is the same as developing one's relationship with God. They are two different things, though. We must not allow the busy schedule of ministry to substitute for spending time with God and growing deeper in our walk with him. I like to tell people that God called us to be something before he called us to do something. He called us to be his disciples, and then he called us to serve him as ministers. Our best serving will come out of our development as disciples. Ignoring our personal relationship with God will cause us to dry up and have nothing to offer people except what we read in some book.

Family. I have met many bivocational ministers who struggled with the feeling that they were neglecting their families. Some have told me they felt called to bivocational ministry but were resisting because they were afraid of how it would impact their families. It is never permissible to neglect one's family in order to serve as a minister of any kind. We must find ways to ensure that we spend time with our families and meet their needs. In *The Healthy Pastor*, I devote an entire chapter to the minister's family and recommend that every bivocational pastor read that chapter.[5]

Church Responsibilities. Being bivocational does not mean it is permissible to provide second-rate ministry, and most bivocational ministers recognize that. Admittedly, though, I have met some bivocational ministers who viewed their work as a Sunday job. It was a way for them to earn extra income, and if they weren't doing that, they might well be working some other job on the weekend. However, most bivocational ministers see their work as a call of God on their lives, and they are as committed to that call as their fully-funded colleagues. They work diligently to provide pastoral care to their congregations, reach out to their communities, prepare quality sermons, and provide leadership to their churches. The biggest danger for most bivocational ministers is that they are more likely sacrifice the other four areas to ensure they provide quality ministry to their churches.

Second Job. I have found that bivocational ministers work in just about every field imaginable. I have met police officers, factory workers, educators (in both public schools and higher education), local politicians, salespeople, business owners, heavy-machine operators, and some even worked jobs that were a little suspect. I once talked to a bivocational pastor whose other employment was dealing cards at a casino in Nevada. Some bivocational ministers work full time at their other jobs; some are part time. Some have to punch a time clock while others enjoy more flexible schedules. The one thing they all have in common is that their jobs require a certain number of hours a week, which means those hours are not available for any other purpose. For most of my bivocational pastorate, I was an hourly factory worker who punched a time card and was required to put in a forty-hour week in the factory. That automatically removed those forty hours from my weekly schedule, plus the commuting time I had.

Self-Care. This fifth area is the one that most ministers, whether bivocational or fully funded, struggle with the most. We are not good at taking care of ourselves. There are so many people with so many different needs and demands that we often sacrifice personal well-being to meet those other needs. Ignoring our own needs long enough can lead to serious problems with physical, emotional, and spiritual health. I recently talked to a bivocational pastor who had fallen into this trap, and he admitted to me that he was on the verge of burnout and about to leave the ministry. We talked for a long time about his years of neglecting his own needs in order to serve others, and I reminded him that self-care is not selfish; it is stewardship of the resources God has given each of us. After our coaching session, he approached his congregation and shared with them the conversation he'd had with me, and they entered a discussion about increasing his vacation time and giving him a three-month sabbatical so he could recharge his emotional batteries.

Self-Esteem Issues

In 2004 I conducted a survey among the bivocational pastors serving in my denomination. A few ministers expressed bitterness at being bivocational. Some were angry they had spent time in seminary and were unable to find a church position that could pay a salary that would support their families. Others were frustrated at the lack of respect they experienced from fully-funded ministers and their denominational leaders.

Perhaps the biggest self-esteem issue comes from the size of the churches many bivocational ministers serve. In the United States, we tend to measure success by numbers. Larger churches represent greater success in ministry. A bivocational pastor serving a church of fifty people may well wonder what is wrong with him when a fellow seminary classmate is already serving a multi-staff church with thousands of attenders. Such comparisons can be hard on one's ego. We can speak all the standard rhetoric about the importance of being faithful where we are, but we are still human beings, and seeing such contrasts can play games with one's self-esteem. Before long, the bivocational minister may begin to question why God doesn't seem to bless his ministry when his classmate's church is growing so fast.

It is important for bivocational ministers to remember that they may not be full-time pastors, but they are full-time ministers. There is never a time when the bivocational minister is not a minister, even if he or she is at the second job. One time our church clerk was filling out the annual reports for our denomination, and she came to the section on the form that asked if I was part time or full time. She wasn't sure how to answer, so she came to ask me what to put down. I responded that I was a full-time bivocational minister. She complained that the form didn't offer that as an option. I told her to mark whichever category she wanted to because I knew what I was. It didn't bother me that I was bivocational or that our denomination did not know how to recognize or capture that information. My self-worth was not connected to the size of the church I served or whether I served as a bivocational minister or a fully-funded minister. Unfortunately, this is an issue for some bivocational ministers.

Lack of Support

It did bother me that during my pastorate there were few resources developed especially for the bivocational church and its leadership. That is why I wrote my first book and why I continue to write today, focusing on issues related to small-church and bivocational ministry. There are also few workshops offered that specifically address the issues and challenges of bivocational and small-church ministry. I am happy to say that some judicatories and denominations are now beginning to address this, but it remains a problem in many others.

A few years ago I was asked to speak about bivocational ministry at a national gathering of pastors. In the two-day event, I was scheduled to present one ninety-minute workshop. Two participants came from several states away and announced during the Q&A time that they only attended because of that workshop. It was the first time they could remember their denomination ever offering something directly related to bivocational ministry. Bivocational pastors are hungry for encouragement and material they can use.

Unique Challenges of Small-Church Ministry

Bivocational ministers often serve in small churches; and, as every minister knows, the challenges of the church become the challenges of the pastor. Small churches are not simply miniature versions of large churches. Everything taught at a church conference cannot always be downsized and made to fit in small-church contexts. People who think that simply do not understand small or bivocational churches, and bivocational ministers who attend such events often find themselves frustrated when they are unable to implement the great ideas they heard when they return to their churches. Bivocational churches have a culture that is very much their own, and not everyone can serve in such churches.

A good number of seminary students today come from large, suburban churches, and they expect to serve in similar settings when they graduate from seminary.[6] Unfortunately, many find that their first ministry after seminary is in a small-church setting, often in places that make becoming bivocational necessary. Making matters worse for the ministers (and the churches), they often find that their seminary educations did not prepare them for the small-church setting.[7]

Poor Self-Esteem

Small churches often do not feel good about themselves. They commonly experience rapid pastoral turnover, causing them to wonder what is so bad about them that no minister wants to stay. They are usually churches with aging members who struggle to attract new and younger members. In many cases, even what children they have in the church do not remain there when they marry. Due to limited finances, the building may not be in good repair and may be dated in appearance. All these issues can cause a small church to feel like it is failing God.

Small churches that used to be much larger can also feel like they have failed. How often do you see congregations of forty people sitting in a church sanctuary built to hold a couple hundred people? It's a common problem today, and such churches often struggle with their sense of self-worth.

The church I pastored had a sanctuary that would hold approximately 100 people. At one time it probably would have held 150, but years earlier the back of the sanctuary had been portioned off to add some Sunday school classes. I was told by longtime members that they could remember when the church was full for Sunday services, and in the summertime, the windows were propped open, and people sat around the sides of the church to listen to the sermon and to sing. When I began my ministry there, the church was down to about thirty people. A number of years earlier the U.S. Army purchased thousands of acres of land near the church for a munitions testing facility. Everyone who lived on that property had to move, and the Army erected a fence around the property. Many of the church members who were forced to move never returned to that church, and attendance immediately plummeted. It was nothing the church had done, but the morale in that church was quite low when I began my pastorate there.

Family Dynamics

Small churches are often referred to as family churches because they may be made up of only a few families—and sometimes only one. Any problem in one of the families often spills over into the church, creating additional problems for the bivocational minister. I know of two churches that had significant problems when family members took different sides on some family-related issues. The pastors of these churches each found themselves in the middle of a family fight that threatened to disrupt the church. Such dynamics can occur in large churches with little impact on the church, but when it happens in the bivocational church, it can often lead to serious issues.

Resistance to Change

I know of few churches that are excited about change, but smaller churches are often especially resistant to any efforts to change them or any aspect of their church life. A minister who presents change is considered by some to be saying that something is wrong with the way the church functions. Longtime members may feel their important traditions are being threatened. Others have been in their churches for many years and have settled into their roles there. Change threatens to take away their established roles or positions in the church, so any change will be strongly resisted. Any pastor who has a vision for the church to be something other than it is in its current state will either have to settle for a long, slow process of gradual changes, or spend the short time he or she is likely to be at the church as a frustrated human being.

It would be a mistake to view bivocational ministers as less talented, less gifted individuals. It would also be a mistake to think that God's call on their lives is less than the call a fully-funded minister experiences. These dedicated ministers are doing kingdom work in their churches, and their numbers are going to continue to increase in most, if not all, denominations over the next several years.

If you are a judicatory minister, I challenge you to embrace your bivocational ministers. Get to know them and their families. Spend some time listening to their hearts. Visit their churches, even those that don't support your denomination very well. There may be a good reason for their poor support, but you won't know it if you don't spend some time with them.

If you are a bivocational minister yourself, seek out an advocate—whether someone higher in your denominational or church structure, or a fully-funded ministerial mentor, or even another bivocational minster—whom you can talk to, learn with and from, and share your needs with.

Coaching is one option that provides a context to help ministers address the challenges they face. Bivocational ministers need encouragement and acceptance. They need someone to come alongside them who appreciates what they do and the sacrifices they make. They need someone who will listen to their needs and offer practical suggestions for self-development tactics they can use to meet those needs. Many of them need a coach.

CHAPTER TWO

UNDERSTANDING COACHING AND SELF-COACHING

Coaching is best understood as a tool to help people get from where they are to where they want to be. We naturally think of sports when we think of coaching. But coaching today is more than drawing up plays and strategies. The most successful coaches know that the mental aspect of the game is just as important as, if not more than, the physical aspect.

A few years ago, I took some golfing lessons. In our first few sessions, my pro spent more time talking about the mental aspect of the game than about the mechanics. In golf, it is important to be able to see what you want to accomplish before you ever start your swing.

Many businesses today also see the importance of coaching, especially for their higher levels of management. Major corporations often include a personal coach as one of the perks offered to upper management. These are not physical coaches; they are executive coaches who can help managers make the best possible decisions.

As has often been the case, the religious world has been slower to grasp the importance of something the rest of the world has understood for several years. Coaching can be a great tool to use to assist persons in ministry positions.

Coaching lets people see a vision of a better future and helps them make changes in how they live and function so that they make that vision a reality. Coaching helps people who are stuck around an issue or in a way of behaving by providing them with new tools and approaches that propel them out of their rut. Those new tools and approaches enable them to behave more effectively in their lives and at work.[1]

The question is sometimes raised: What is the difference between coaching and consulting, counseling, or mentoring? Actually, there are several differences, and it's important to understand them if we want to coach ourselves or get the greatest gain from having a coach.

Coaches Are Not Experts

Mentors or consultants are normally seen as experts in their particular fields. They may have years of experience and/or advanced degrees that relate to working in those areas. They are often called in to solve problems. They are given certain information and are expected to identify and recommend solutions. Consultants or mentors can only tell their clients what they themselves know from their experiences consulting or mentoring in their fields, and that is the limiting factor.

A coach is not an expert and is not expected to know everything related to any particular field. With a basic knowledge of coaching, however, a good coach can assist a bivocational minister, a business leader, a salesman, a farmer, and people looking for solutions to some of life's challenges as well as a whole host of others. Coaching begins with the premise that the person being coached already knows the steps he or she needs to take but for some reason is reluctant to take those steps. Coaching does not give answers, as would mentoring or consulting; a coach asks powerful questions that challenge the person being coached to find the answers from within himself or herself.

Actually, the field expert in a coaching relationship is the person being coached, which is why one can often self-coach. You know you better than anyone else. You know your situation better than anyone else ever could. You know how your situation impacts your ability to move forward, how it impacts your family, your church, your health, and every other area of your life. Often, you already know the options you have in any situation. The only thing you need is help bringing those options to the surface and implementing them.

A good coach asks powerful questions to help the person being coached identify those solutions then holds the person accountable for implementation. These questions usually begin with what, when, who, and how. Let me give you a few examples to help get you started, but please realize these are not all inclusive.

- Of the various issues facing you right now, what seems to be the most urgent?
- Out of this situation, what is the best thing that could happen?
- That's one option; what are some others?
- Whom or what do you need to succeed?
- What could prevent you from succeeding?
- Whom do you need to talk to about this situation? When will you do that?
- Who will hold you accountable to take the actions you've identified?

Many coaches try to avoid asking *why* questions because why often implies fault or blame. Think back to your childhood. If it was like mine, having a parent ask, "Why did you do this?" usually wasn't a good thing. There may be times when you do want to understand why a decision was made, but even then, a simple rephrase of the typical *why* question will erase the negative implications of blame and introduce a process of intentional reflection. Such a question might be, *What circumstances or train of thought led you to believe this was a good option, solution, or decision?* Good coaches never beat up the people they are coaching, and you should not beat yourself up either when you are coaching yourself. There's a lot to be said for a well-worded and well-timed question to help someone else or yourself think through difficult situations.

Coaches Focus on the Future

As I have shared elsewhere, many years ago I personally experienced a period of clinical depression. In addition to medication, I spent a year with a pastoral counselor. Like most counselors, she spent a great deal of time looking to the past for the cause of my depression. Coaches, on the other hand, do not spend much time looking to the past; instead, a good coach looks to the future. A coach meets the individual being coached where that person is in his or her life journey and tries to help that individual identify the things needed to move forward.[2]

It should be noted that there are times when the person being coached needs the services of a counselor. There may be trauma from past experiences that is responsible for holding captive the person being coached, making it impossible for him or her to move forward. There are also times when the person being coached cannot be helped by asking powerful questions. He or she may not have the proper experience or knowledge of the situation to know what a good course of action might be. No amount of questions can pull something out of someone that isn't there to begin with. Such persons need the assistance of mentors or consultants to help fill in the missing information. A capable coach watches for signs that indicate that something more than coaching is needed, and will refer the person to someone who is qualified to assist.

During my struggle with depression, I could not have been helped by a coach. There were physiological issues that needed to be addressed with medication, which required a physician. There were emotional and psychological issues from my past that needed to be addressed and processed with the services of a trained counselor who could help me make sense of those issues and offer assistance as I attempted to address them.

Coaches must be aware of their limitations and be willing to refer people to the appropriate professionals when necessary. In my own coaching relationships, I have occasionally felt that the person I was coaching showed signs of depression. I pointed that out to those individuals and encouraged them to seek professional assistance. Coaching would have limited success in such situations because the people would have struggled to process what we were trying to do through coaching due to the depression that clouded their thinking.

As you coach yourself, always focus on the future. It's important to understand the past, but there is nothing you can do about it now. Any mistakes made in the past are history. So, unfortunately, are your successes. Our challenge is always to live in the present while looking toward the future. I always found great encouragement in the apostle Paul's comments in Philippians. After reviewing his past with readers, he writes that he is "forgetting those things which are behind and reaching forward to those things which are ahead, I press toward the goal for the prize of the upward call of God in Christ Jesus" (3:13b-14). Personally, I find that taking such an approach to life and ministry is much more productive than spending time regretting past decisions or focusing on previous mistakes.

Review again the examples of powerful questions. All the questions look forward, not backward. They are designed to help you get unstuck and moving again, not trying to figure out why you were stuck in the first place. These types of questions will help you identify the steps you need to take in order to achieve the goals you've determined for your life and ministry. By their very nature, they will keep you looking and moving forward with your life, and this is the purpose of coaching, whether you self-coach or bring in someone to help you.

Coaches Develop People, Not Solve Problems

Mentors, counselors, and consultants come in to solve problems. Coaches attempt to help the persons they are coaching to develop their problem-solving skills. As Tony Stoltzfus explains, "We can build people or we can solve problems. Transformational coaching is about building people. This approach is a far more powerful method of producing leaders, and yields long-term results."[3] Elsewhere he explains why this is important.

I'm much more interested in helping people become great deci-sion-makers than in helping them make a right decision. If they make a good choice, I've influenced that one situation. But if I help them grow in their ability to make great choices, *I've affected every decision they make for the rest of their life.*[4]

The ability to make choices is as critical to the success of bivoca-tional ministers as it is to anyone in a leadership position. Virtually every day they are confronted with a host of choices. They feel the pull of the needs of their families, their churches, their other employers, their relationship with God, and their own personal needs. Each one of these makes demands on their time. Bivocational ministry is a constant balancing act that requires making good choices. A coach can help bivocational ministers make good choices, as well as grow in their ability to eventually make good decisions without a coach's assistance.

Can one self-coach and develop better decision-making abilities in the process? I believe so, because many people have never developed a system for making important decisions. Some over-analyze every issue. They continually feel they must have one more piece of information before they can make a decision. Or, to spiritualize their dilemma, they need to "pray about it some more." While there is always a need to pray about the decisions we make, there is also a time when we need to just make a decision. Those who consistently over-analyze every decision are procrastinators who fear making the wrong decision. Let me help you with this: *You will make poor decisions.* Not every decision you make will prove to be a good one. That's why pencils come with an eraser, or, perhaps more appropriate in the twenty-first century, it's why computers have delete keys. Mistakes can be corrected. Though they may harm you in the short term, it is often the case that not making a decision can be more costly than making the wrong decision.

The other thing decision makers need to realize is that you will never have all the information you need. There will always be more data you could consider, but to continually look for that data may make whatever decision you finally do make irrelevant because the need has already passed. You make decisions based on the best information you have at the time, and if new data becomes available that means your decision needs to be tweaked, then you can change it.

What is critical is that persons in leadership, including bivocational ministers, have a process by which they make decisions. Again, consider how developing coaching questions similar to the examples provided earlier can help that process. You can write down the decision that confronts you and begin to ask applicable questions. Systematically work your way down your list of questions until you feel comfortable with the answer you are getting. You can ask others those same questions to get their input as well.

When I coached the persons in section two, they often wanted to ask me the questions so I would tell them what they needed to do. As a coach, I could not do that and still help them develop their own decision-making abilities. Instead, I asked them questions to force them to think through the issues that confronted them. The more questions I asked, the deeper we got into the issues until they finally had *Aha!* moments when the answers became clear. That is what you want to do when you self-coach. Keep going deeper in your challenge through the questions you ask about the situation until the correct response becomes obvious to you. As you consistently use that approach to all the challenges you have, you will continue to grow in your decision-making abilities.

A Strategy for Self-Coaching

Most things seem to work better if you have a system to follow. If you want to coach yourself, it is best to have a strategy that is likely to lead to a more successful outcome. While nothing in this section is written in stone, this is a system that will help most people.

The first thing you must do is identify one issue you need to address. This can often be the most difficult step you'll take. When I coach someone, one of my first questions is, "What is the best use of our time today?" Sometimes the person being coached identifies one topic immediately while other times he or she might list half a dozen things. I then ask, "Of all the issues, which one is your top priority?" You cannot coach five different things at one time; you must identify the one that seems to be the biggest challenge at the moment and work through it before addressing the next issue.

Once you identify the most pressing issue in your life, write it down on a piece of paper, and then begin to list the reasons it is a challenge. What problems does it create? How does it hold you back from moving on? How does it disrupt your life or your relationships with other people? The more reasons you can list, the better you'll be able to address it.

Next, write out some questions to help you in the coaching process. You may want to use some of those I listed above. You'll find many more questions in the case studies in the next section that may be helpful to your specific situation. Methodically, work your way through those questions. It may be that one thing will bring more questions to mind, and that is good too. Remember that these questions should help you move forward, not dwell on the past, and assist you in finding solutions that will enable that forward movement.

As you begin to identify solutions, they should lead to action steps. Perhaps you need to talk to someone about a specific issue. Maybe there is some training you need to help you with the challenge. There may be some resources you need to acquire. Good coaching will always lead to action, so it is vital that you identify the best course to take to overcome the issue.

The final step in the strategy is to find someone to hold you accountable. You must share your plan of action with someone who will help keep your feet to the fire. Without accountability, it is too easy to plan to do your action step sometime in the future, and we know how that often turns out. You need to set a deadline for when you will take that action, and have someone who will call you on that date and ask how it went.

This strategy will take time, but as I often tell people in my workshops, "Whatever problem you face likely didn't occur last night, and it's not going to be fixed tomorrow." My coaching clients typically spend six one-hour sessions with me over a three-month period. In addition, there is work they must do between the sessions as they follow through on the various action steps the need to take, which they identified in our sessions.

Three months, in the proper perspective, is not too much time to allot to overcome a challenge that holds you back from advancing in your life or ministry. It may be quicker for some while others need more than three months, but at least you're moving forward. I've known people who worried about the same issue for years and never did anything to resolve it. Whatever time it takes you in the self-coaching process is an investment in your future, and that's the best investment you'll ever have.

This book is written to help bivocational ministers coach themselves through many of the challenges they face. The case studies in section two represent some of the most common issues that confront bivocational ministers today. However, there may be times when ministers are so stuck, so confused, so frustrated, that they are unable to coach themselves through their challenges. If that happens to you, you may want to consider bringing in a coach.

The good news is that this is often a short-term process. I have never coached anyone beyond six sessions over a three-month period. By that time, they have usually begun to develop some momentum in their lives and ministries and been ready to move forward without me. Most of these individuals had also developed better problem-solving skills as a result of our sessions, and were able to self-coach in the future.

If you do need to seek a coach, there are certain qualities to look for, and you yourself will likely give some indications that you are ready to be coached. Frankly, not everyone is a good candidate for coaching. Recognizing the indicators will help you know if now is a time in your life when coaching will help you.

Qualities of a Good Coach

Like any profession, some people go into coaching who lack the basic skills or temperament to be good coaches. Even if someone is a good coach, that does not mean that particular person is a good match for everyone. I've gone to a dentist and decided not to go back because I wasn't comfortable with his approach. I've gone to a barber shop and knew after the first haircut I would not be back. I've changed tax advisors when I felt misunderstood. Similarly, not every coach, no matter how competent, will be a good match for every person.

Most coaches and persons wanting to be coached will know during the initial conversation whether they feel comfortable with each other and want to pursue the relationship. Neither the coach nor the person wanting to be coached should feel bad if either one decides this relationship is not one they want to pursue. It may also be that they decide to continue the relationship but later realize it's not working as they thought it would, and that's okay too. It's never too late to break off a coaching relationship.

One question that often arises is the question of certification. Currently, there are no licensing requirements for coaches. Anyone can claim to be a coach without any training or credentials. There are several organizations that offer coaching training and certify persons as coaches at various levels. However, certification does not guarantee that the person is a competent coach, nor does it guarantee that a coach will be a good fit for someone seeking to be coached. I have known some excellent coaches who did not pursue certification, and I've met a few certified coaches whom I felt were, at best, average. My own personal situation is that I have received training in coaching techniques, but I do not currently meet the number of hours of coaching experience that is required by most organizations for certification.

Good Coaches See Value in People

John Whitmore observes that an effective coach will be one who sees people in terms of their potential, not their performance.[5] This will require that the coach be someone who has a genuine interest in the person and his or her success. Such a coach will look beyond the current situation or issues and help the person being coached to do the same. The best coaches help those they serve identify their dreams and the steps it will take to achieve those dreams, and they walk with them on the journey toward fulfilling them.

I often tell people in workshops that when I began my pastorate at Hebron I had no education beyond high school, no pastoral experience, and was even missing a front tooth that broke off about a week before my interview with the church. Yet they were willing to take a chance on me. That may have been as much desperation on their part as anything, but no congregation could have been more patient with someone who had a strong desire to pastor but little else to offer a church. I had been there for a couple of years when one of the longtime members told me as he left the service, "You know, you're starting to become a pretty good preacher!" For some reason, that small church saw potential in me and allowed me time to grow into that potential. They saw value in me that other churches might not have seen, and as a result, we enjoyed a great twenty-year ministry there.

The same thing will be true of a good coach. The best coaches will see the potential in every person they coach, and will be committed to helping those individuals live up to their potential. Look for a coach who will value you as an individual and see the potential God has given you.

Good Coaches Are Good Communicators

An important aspect of communication is listening, and the best coaches are good listeners. Persons being coached will usually tell the coach what the primary issues are, but the coach must actively listen. Active listening involves giving feedback to ensure that the coach has correctly understood what is being said. A coach who fails to practice active listening runs the risk of attempting to address issues not being raised.

Another important element of communicating for the coach is to ask powerful questions that force the person being coached to think through the issues. Open-ended questions require the person being coached to go deeper and focus on the root causes of the issues.[6] The person being coached may have preferred to stay on surface issues in the past and not probe beneath to identify the roots of the problems, but until this is done, no permanent solution will be found. Some coaches believe these questions are so important they should make up half of the coaching conversation.[7]

Good Coaches Encourage People

People often turn to a coach because they feel stuck. Perhaps they have run into roadblocks and don't know how to move forward. They may have been in that situation for some time and are greatly discouraged. Some of the people I have coached were almost ready to leave the ministry because the level of frustration was so high. Such people are looking for someone to come alongside them who is optimistic, positive, and able to offer encouragement. Good coaches reflect all three of these qualities.

Hardly a week goes by that I do not receive a phone call, email, or personal contact from a discouraged bivocational minister. They are frustrated with the lack of progress in their churches; they are frustrated with the amount of time and energy they have left for their families; they often wonder if they are wasting their time trying to minister to people who don't seem to appreciate anything they do.

I don't know any group of people in more need of encouragement than bivocational ministers. That's why, in every workshop I lead and every meeting I have with bivocational ministers, I spend a good portion of time letting them know that what they are doing is important kingdom work. I try to encourage them every way I can.

I am often amazed how far a little encouragement can go. I really shouldn't be surprised if I stop and think back to my own bivocational pastorate. Just a smile and a brief word of appreciation was often enough to wipe away a week's worth of frustration and inspire me to keep doing what God called me to do. A good coach can do the same thing in a bivocational minister's life.

Good Coaches Demand Accountability

All this talk about the importance of coaches believing in the value of the people being coached, and the need for coaches to be positive, encouraging people does not mean coaches do not hold people accountable. Accountability is a key element in a coaching relationship. Every coaching session should end with some specific actions the person being coached will take before the next session. The next session will begin with a review of those steps and a report from the person being coached as to what was done. If the work was not done, a good coach will want to know why. People who do not do what they commit to must be challenged, and if they continue to fail to keep their commitments, a good coach will question whether to continue the coaching relationship. A coaching relationship can only succeed if the person being coached is willing to make commitments and keep them. If the person being coached is unwilling or unable to do this, there is no need to continue the relationship. Holding people accountable may seem harsh, but it is really a reflection of the value the coach places on the person being coached.

I once took a class in Bible college that did not involve any exams. The professor required three papers. On the first day of class, he explained that each paper was due on the date listed in the syllabus, and if the paper was late, we would receive a zero. No excuse was acceptable. We knew well in advance what the requirements of the course were, and if we didn't like it, we could drop the class. He then explained that, as ministers, we would be making commitments to people, and they would expect us to honor those commitments.

For instance, pastors should know that every Sunday they must be prepared to preach a sermon. Regardless of what happens during the week, people will gather in church on Sunday morning expecting to hear a sermon. They are not interested in hearing our excuses about how the pastor didn't have time that week to prepare one. That college professor was preparing us for the real world of ministry. For the same reasons, coaches who do not hold people accountable do them a disservice.

This can be a challenge for the person who self-coaches. Who will hold us accountable for the decisions we make? One of the keys of coaching is that there must be a plan of action that defines what will be done, by whom, and when. If there is no action, there has not been quality coaching. If we coach ourselves, we must bring someone into our plans who will hold us accountable. This could be a spouse, another minister, a denominational leader, or someone else we respect who cares enough about our growth that he or she will hold us accountable.

Good Coaches Are Flexible

In a coaching relationship, the person being coached always sets the agenda. I have thought I knew in advance what would be discussed in a coaching session, only to be surprised by the raising of a completely different issue. This was usually the result of an event that had occurred since our last conversation that had become more critical than what had been previously discussed. I had to be flexible enough to allow the session to go in a different direction than I anticipated.

Qualities of a Good Coaching Client

Just as not every coach is a good match for every person, not everyone expressing an interest in being coached is ready for a coaching relationship. I have found that the best persons to coach are those who are dissatisfied with situations in their lives but uncertain how to resolve them. This does not mean that only people having problems seek a coach. The best candidates for coaching may be those who are doing well but believe they can do even better. These are often the ones most motivated to move forward with their lives.

If you are interested in working with a coach or doing some self-coaching, there are some questions you should ask yourself.

- What is your motivation for wanting to be coached? Do you have some specific goals you want to pursue, or do you need a coach to help give you direction?
- Are you willing to make at least a three-month commitment to the process?
- Are you willing to be accountable to the things you will commit to in your coaching sessions? Every good coach will end each session by asking you to commit to doing something you have identified as needing to be accomplished. Some people enjoy *identifying* things they should be doing; they don't always enjoy actually *doing* them in a timely manner. If you self-coach, you must be disciplined enough to make commitments and hold

yourself accountable to them, or you will not be successful in your efforts.

- How well do you respond to feedback, both positive and negative? I hate when I ask myself a question and then don't like the answer, but for a successful coaching experience, you will have to be completely honest with yourself or your coach.

- Are you open to new ways of thinking and doing? Some people seek a coach hoping to find someone who will reinforce their current beliefs and actions, and such people are seldom coachable.

- Are you looking for a quick fix to your problems? If so, coaching may not be for you. Coaching does not offer cookie-cutter approaches to solving problems but seeks solutions to specific issues. Because it is contextual, it can take a period of time before the person being coached identifies the problems.

- Can you make time in your busy schedule for a coaching relationship? As a church leader, your time is already in high demand. At a minimum, you should count on at least two sixty-minute contacts with your coach each month. Plus, you will have assignments to work on between those contacts. You will likely not have a good coaching experience if you have to squeeze a coaching relationship into a schedule that is already too full.

- While this is not an issue for one who self-coaches, those who seek a coach must consider whether they can afford the financial expense. Though executive coaches sometimes charge $800 or more per month, most coaches who work with ministers have a much lower fee. In particular, my fees are less than half that amount, but there is a financial cost involved that you should discuss with your potential coach in your introductory session. I encourage you to see the cost as an investment rather than an expense, however. Remember, investing in yourself is one investment you will never lose, no matter what the economy does. It may be possible to enjoy the benefits of having a coach without any financial expense. Some judicatories now offer coaching to their bivocational ministers at no cost.

- Are you ready to begin now? Don't start a coaching relationship if there are major distractions in your life, such as a serious illness in the family or other events on the horizon that you know will require much of your time and energy. If such an event occurs after you begin your coaching relationship, ask your coach for some time off until the event is resolved. Good coaches will always readily agree to let you deal with pressing problems then return to the coaching relationship.

If you can answer yes to each of these questions, you are probably ready to begin a self-coaching endeavor or coaching relationship.

One coach can easily serve four or five bivocational ministers at a time; coaching can be done over the phone, resulting in less travel time; and it has been proven to be an effective way to develop problem-solving skills. For those persons who are ready, coaching will often prove to be the quickest way for them to go from where they are in life to where they want to be.

Coaching should not be the only tool or resource a denomination offers its bivocational ministers, but it should absolutely be included in the mix. It has been proven to be an effective tool in the business world and the sports world, and it is proving to be effective with church leaders, both bivocational and fully funded.

SECTION 2

THE SCENARIOS

The chapters that comprise this section will explore some common issues faced by bivocational ministers and how these issues were addressed through coaching relationships I had with each individual. We will, of course, maintain absolute confidentiality and refer to the persons being coached by letters in alphabetical order. Many, but not all, of the issues discussed in this section were raised during my doctorate project while I coached five ministers serving in various churches across the United States and Canada. Other issues come from other coaching relationships I have had with bivocational ministers at various times. Each of the issues has been selected because it is common among bivocational ministers.

Judicatory leaders should also find the chapters in this section helpful. If you have bivocational ministers serving in your districts, there is a good chance some of them face the problems addressed herein. These chapters will give you some new tools you can use as you assist these pastors. As a side note, the final chapter of the book is written especially for judicatory leaders. You may want to skip to that chapter before reading these, or you can go ahead and read these chapters first.

Before proceeding, let me share how I begin a coaching relationship and gather information that will be helpful to the relationship. There are some things I require each person to provide before our first session. One is a Life Satisfaction Indicator, which is a form that forces individuals to think through various categories of life and decide their level of satisfaction in each category. The categories include personal spiritual life and growth; the quality of relationships they have with family, friends, and others; their own well-being, both physically and emotionally; their financial well-being; and numerous other issues. The areas where clients indicate dissatisfaction often get addressed in some of the coaching sessions, especially if they are areas that correlate to ministry or seem to inform some of the decisions being made in the person's ministry. The form I use for the Life Satisfaction Indicator is adapted from one presented during my coaching training, but you can develop one that fits your style and gathers the information you find helpful.

I also require each person I coach to complete an online assessment that evaluates spiritual gifts in combination with personality types. It generates a report of approximately thirty-five pages, which I ask the individuals to email me prior to our first session. The particular report I ask them to complete does charge a small fee ($15 at the time of this writing), but the return on the investment outweighs the cost, considering how much people learn about themselves. For many of the people I coach, this is the first time they have received an assessment of this nature, and it often reveals quite a lot to them. Many of them tell me their spouses feel the assessments contain accurate descriptions of their gifts and personality types. Sometimes I too get useful information from these evaluations that I can then use in our coaching sessions, but the real value lies in what they learn about themselves and how God created them. I especially recommend this resource to anyone who wants to self-coach. Various questionnaires of this nature and other types can be downloaded in the Questionnaires section at *www.uniquelyyou.com.*

Finally, I require each person to sign an agreement to formalize the coaching relationship. I usually ask for a minimum of three months (six sessions) because it takes time to develop a relationship, and a certain level of closeness and understanding are essential for successful coaching experiences. The agreement clearly spells out the expectations for both the coach and the person being coached so there is no confusion.

Of course, you do not have to use forms or follow the process I use. There are thousands of coaches, and all of them have their own techniques that have proven useful. I share my own only to demonstrate what has been helpful in my coaching journey. Chances are, as you continue to coach others, you will develop some techniques that prove to be more helpful to you than others. The important thing is for you to identify the tools that will make your coaching more helpful to those you serve.

CHAPTER THREE

FAMILY CHALLENGES

Session 1

Pastor A indentified several challenges in our initial conversation and on his Life Satisfaction Indicator. He scored very low in his relationship with his wife, fun and hobbies, and indicated he had no friends or social life outside the church. He felt little support from his wife for his ministry. Finally, both he and his wife were dissatisfied with the physical condition of their home; they both felt the desire to make maintenance improvements. At the core of his problems were his own doubts about the effectiveness of his ministry. He felt that if he could just become a better pastor, the other things might fall into place.

Coaching should always be driven by the agenda of the person being coached, so I asked which of the many issues he articulated was the most pressing. He eventually identified his biggest challenge as his lack of a strong personal spiritual life. Like many pastors, much of his reading was for sermon preparation. He admitted to spending little time on personal spiritual growth. I asked what would hinder him from developing a time for his own spiritual development. He was able to identify two primary hindrances: scheduling, and finding something suitable to read to begin. Interestingly enough, while we discussed this, he noticed a book on his bookshelf that had been given him that he had never read. He decided then and there to begin by reading that book, which took care of one obstacle.

Like many bivocational ministers, his schedule was pretty tight, but he was able to identify one hour on Monday nights that would work for him. He invited his wife to hold him accountable and knew that I would begin our next session by asking how that reading affected his spiritual development.

Session Two

As we began our second coaching session, he told me his devotional time was going well. He had already purchased some more books to read when he completed the first one, and he felt less stressed. He identified his church's desire to grow as the topic he wanted to explore in this session.

I asked what could be done in his community to encourage people to begin attending his church. He identified five things, none of which would be difficult for a church his size. Further conversation led him to identify three questions he would ask at an upcoming board meeting. He recognized that growth wasn't his responsibility alone, and he wanted to challenge the church board and congregation to ask themselves some questions about their own commitment to growth.

One thing that impressed me in this session was how quickly he identified specific things that could be done by his congregation to encourage growth. A primary tenet of coaching asserts that people usually already know the answers to the questions they have; they just don't always know how to access those answers. After a few key questions, this pastor was able to identify several good options to explore with the rest of the church.

Before ending this session, Pastor A admitted some frustration that his judicatory leader would not return his phone calls. He wanted assistance in trying to transform his church but felt that some of his denominational leaders were not willing to work with him or the church. I encouraged him to continue trying to contact that leader.

Session Three

Pastor A was excited as our third coaching session began. He had made contact with the judicatory leader who then attended their board meeting and discussed with them some things the judicatory could do to help them grow. The board decided to participate in an eight-week emphasis on evangelism and church vitality that their denomination would be offering later that year. In addition, they were going to begin a small group that would reach out to young couples, and the pastor wanted to focus this session on five specific concerns he had about that group.

We explored each concern individually. I asked guiding questions, and he identified steps actions he could take. In a one-hour phone conversation, he was able to identify three things he could do to resolve his concerns. His assignment before our next session was to complete all three steps.

Session Four

In our first coaching conversation, Pastor A was discouraged, but as we began this fourth session, he was a completely changed person. He had started work on his house, his wife was much happier and more supportive of his ministry, and good things were happening at the church. In fact, so many good things had begun at the church that he was concerned that he and the other leaders would become weary from all the activity.

His focus for this session was to address an upcoming ministry opportunity being presented by his denomination. He and his board were going to attend a presentation on the opportunity that would later be presented to the church, but he wasn't sure the entire board was really in agreement with the direction the church was going. I asked how he could be convinced that everyone was supportive. After some thought, he decided to ask each board member to lead one of the eight sessions that would be presented to the congregation. I followed that response by questioning how he would measure the success of the proposed solution. He responded that if half of the board agreed to lead a session, he would feel positive about the board's commitment.

Session Five

Pastor A was eager to report that every board member had agreed to lead a session as they trained the congregation in the new ministry opportunity. The unanimous support was greatly encouraging to this pastor.

For this session, the pastor wanted help in ministering to a family who had a member diagnosed with a serious illness. The family had a superficial relationship with the church, and the pastor wasn't sure how to approach them. One of my questions was whether there was someone in the church who had the trust of this family and who could accompany the pastor on his first visit. I then asked if there was anywhere he could turn for resources he could use as he ministered to the family. He identified a leader in the church who could serve as a bridge, and he also identified a nearby hospital chaplain who could help him find tools and resources.

Although some bivocational ministers have advanced degrees, many others have not attended college or seminary. These pastors often struggle with the confidence they need to minister in difficult situations. By helping Pastor A identify someone who could help him find resources to make him more comfortable in reaching out to this family, I helped Pastor A realize he didn't have to minister alone. He had allies who would be willing to give him the benefit of their education and experience, which seemed to inspire more confidence, as it often does. In my own bivocational pastorate, once I became willing to go to other pastors and professionals with some of my questions, I became much more confident in ministering to individuals and families going through difficult times.

Session Six

Pastor A was a few minutes late to our phone conference for the sixth session. When he called, he was excited because some men from the church had come to his house to help with some repairs. They had approached him the previous Sunday to ask how they could help, and their willingness and hard work was a great encouragement to Pastor A and his wife.

Although this was our last session, he did not want to address anything new. We spent our time talking about the new confidence he had in ministry and in his own abilities as a minister. He had visited the family we discussed in the fifth session and begun a relationship with them. Pastor A was surprised to note that every challenge he listed in our initial session had been turned around in only three months' time. He learned he was not alone in ministry. He learned the importance of ministers having time for their own spiritual development and the importance of taking time for family and self-care. As we ended our final conversation, I encouraged him to remember the lessons learned from the coaching experience when new challenges arose in the future.

In a written statement he made reviewing our coaching relationship, he expressed that the greatest benefit he received was the affirmation of God's call on his life to bivocational ministry. His confidence in himself as a minister had grown considerably, and that confidence in turn allowed him to be a much more effective minister.

Debrief

It should be noted that coaches cannot always expect to see such a dramatic turnaround in only six sessions. Pastor A was highly motivated to receive coaching, and he was faithful to complete his assignments between each session. He also served a church that was open to change and committed to growth. Unfortunately, not all pastors serve in such churches.

However, although Pastor A was unusual in some ways, his situation is common among bivocational ministers. He was tired, frustrated, facing problems in the church and at home, and wasn't sure of his own ministerial capabilities. If he had tried to address each of his problems at the same time, it is likely he would have felt overwhelmed and may have given up. By focusing on one thing at a time, and allowing him to dictate at each session what his focus would be, he was able to break down his problems to a more manageable size. He could look for solutions to just one problem at a time and work on that for two weeks before having to report back.

As Pastor A grew more confident in ministry, both his congregation and his wife noticed. His board willingly followed his leadership and moved sooner than anticipated to support new initiatives. His wife also became more supportive of his ministry as he took more time for her and their family. The more the church and his family supported his ministry, the more confident he became and the more enjoyable the ministry became. He also became more willing to stretch himself to minister in situations he may have tried to avoid in the past.

CHAPTER FOUR

UNCERTAINTY ABOUT THE CALL TO MINISTRY

Pastor B struggled with his sense of call. His spiritual gift assessment identified his primary gifts to be teaching, prophecy, and evangelism, with pastor/shepherd only one point behind evangelism. His spiritual gifts certainly were in line with those of a pastor. Pastor B's most recent ministry had been as a bivocational youth minister. He resigned the position because the responsibilities had grown to require more time than he could give. Four years prior to the time we began our coaching relationship, Pastor B's wife divorced him, claiming she did not want to be married to a minister. The church he served at that time as a pastor terminated his employment as a result of the divorce.

In our initial conversation, it quickly became obvious that his divorce and the church's response to it had created trust issues with the church. Furthermore, the time demands in his second ministry attempt led to a difficult relationship with the pastor of that church, which made him even more leery of ministry. Pastor B carried a lot of internal pain over his difficult experiences with the church, leading him to struggle with what he perceived to be God's call on his life.

Compounding his problems even more was the knowledge that many churches in his denomination would not consider him for the pastorate due to a divorce he had not initiated. This denomination was the only one he had ever known, and he felt he would have to leave it if he ever returned to pastoral ministry.

On a more positive note, he had remarried and seemed to have a healthy relationship with his wife, who supported his desire to serve in ministry. He had a good relationship with his children from the previous marriage and a good career. Pastor B scored average or higher on nearly all areas on the Life Satisfaction Indicator.

Session One

In our first coaching session, Pastor B wanted to look at the possibility of serving as a bivocational pastor. He wanted to return to a ministry role yet was afraid of being hurt again by a church. He also had a strong fear of failing. Pastor B saw bivocational ministry as a safe way to return to ministry. He also believed a small church might be more open to calling a divorced person as pastor. After discussing the advantages and disadvantages of bivocational ministry for a few minutes, I asked him to identify some roadblocks he could perceive that could make bivocational ministry difficult for him. He was able to list four.

- The church would have to be reasonably close to where he lived. He already drove several miles to work in an effort to remain close to his children from his first marriage. He would not want to move further away from them.
- He noted that a seminary in his community made available a large number of student pastors who often served the smaller churches in the area. That would limit the number of churches that would be interested in a bivocational minister.

- He was uncertain about how his visitation schedule with his children would impact his ability to serve a church.
- Many churches would automatically reject him due to his divorce.

As we concluded the session, I asked him if there were people who supported his call to ministry whom he could talk to about his fears. He identified three people and promised to talk with them before our next session. To address his fears of failure, I asked him to begin reading John Maxwell's book *Failing Forward*,[1] which he agreed to do.

Session Two

Pastor B had talked to the three people about his call to ministry and his fears about returning to ministry. All three agreed that he had been called to ministry but cautioned him to return gradually until he completed some other tasks he had begun. His wife was also concerned about being able to live up to her preconceptions of a pastor's wife. Despite their concerns, he wanted to discuss how he could begin looking for a bivocational church to serve.

I asked him to describe what he would like in a church he pastored. The qualities he listed would be found in many people's ideal church, but I cautioned him that it would not be likely he would find all of them in any one church. I then asked him how he would determine whether a church did possess these qualities, and he admitted he needed some guidance. At that point I switched hats and spent the rest of our time together serving as a mentor, not a coach. We ended that aspect of our conversation by identifying some good questions he could ask a church search committee.

Pastor B had two projects he wanted to complete before our next session. He wanted to work on developing more questions for a pastor search committee, and he wanted to ask his wife to talk to the wife of someone serving in a bivocational ministry position to gain her perspective on the role and expectations of a bivocational pastor's wife.

Session Three

As we began our third session, Pastor B reported he had completed his list of questions and updated his résumé to submit to bivocational churches. His wife had not been able to talk to the wife of a bivocational minister because they realized they didn't know any. I was able to recommend one in his area who had served many years as a bivocational pastor. Pastor B was excited to tell me he had found a new position in his other career that would make it easier for him to serve as a pastor. He saw this as a sign that God still wanted to use him in ministry.

In this session, he wanted to discuss the possibility that a church might want to call more than one person as a bivocational pastor. Although co-pastors are not common in bivocational ministry, I know of some cases where co-pastors have been called because of work schedules. I asked him to name some advantages and disadvantages of bivocational co-pastors, and it was obvious he expected the question because he had a list already developed.

The project to be completed before our next session was for him and his wife to talk to the pastor and wife I recommended to him.

Session Four

Unfortunately, Pastor B and his wife did not complete their task. At first, he claimed he did not have the time to schedule a meeting with the other pastor. He finally admitted that the real reason was his fear of returning to ministry. We spent the remainder of the fourth session discussing those fears.

Since his first wife left him because she did not want to be married to a minister, Pastor B was afraid his current wife might also leave him if he returned to ministry. Although she verbally expressed her support, she did have some concerns about her own ability to be a minister's wife. In response to a question I asked, Pastor B expressed his confidence that God had called him into ministry. At that point he realized that he either had to accept that call or ignore it.

For the remainder of our session, Pastor B wanted to discuss how he could be at one church for a lengthy period of time. His two previous ministry roles had been short term, and he did not want to continue that trend. When I asked him to list some conditions that could lead to a long-term pastorate, he named several.

- A good fit between the church and the minister
- A support system that included family and peers
- A preaching plan
- An ability to develop relationships with church members
- A commitment to staying during the difficult times
- A healthy relationship with his spouse and family
- A commitment to personal growth

As our time drew to a close, he identified three things he would do before our next session. He and his wife would meet with the other minister and his wife; he would look into a local bivocational ministry fellowship that I told him about; and he would talk honestly with his wife about his fears of returning to ministry.

Session Five

Due to conflicting schedules, Pastor B and the other pastor were still not able to make contact, but they had an appointment scheduled for the week following our fifth session. When he talked to his wife about his fears, he found that she completely supported him in his decision to return to ministry. And, since our last session, he'd had the opportunity to fill a pulpit for a vacationing pastor, which excited him and helped him become even more determined to return to ministry.

In this session, Pastor B wanted to focus on his résumé, especially the part about how he should let a church know about his previous divorce. He had been working on this since our last session and asked to read a statement he had written about his divorce. It seemed thorough and honest about how it had occurred, and I encouraged him to include the paragraph with any résumé submissions.

He then wanted to work on wording that would help a church know he was interested in serving as their pastor long term. With my prompting, he developed several possible statements he could use. After a time of prayer, he could select which statement to include.

As this session ended, I reminded Pastor B that our next session would be our last one, and I encouraged him to give careful consideration to what he wanted to address in that session. He was to continue developing his resume, and he promised to keep the appointment with the other pastor.

Session Six

Pastor B was greatly encouraged by his meeting with the other pastor. This individual had served many years as a bivocational minister, and he was open about the mistakes he had made earlier in his ministry, especially ones affecting his family. Pastor B felt he received excellent advice from this pastor.

In this final session, he wanted to know how he could promote bivocational ministry. He had realized through discussion and study that bivocational ministry was becoming increasingly important to the church. He wanted to encourage other bivocational ministers, and he hoped to raise up bivocational ministers from the membership of the church he might serve.

As we concluded our time together, he shared that some of our sessions had been emotionally difficult. He was forced to address issues he had refused to consider in recent years, and he was forced to talk to others about those issues and how they impacted him. However, in the end, he felt he had grown as a result of our time together and that he would now be able to return to ministry. As he reflected on the experience, Pastor B later wrote to me:

> The entire coaching process was difficult work for me, as I was truly seeking to grow and to find God's direction for my life. The Lord used this opportunity to help me move from a point of insecurity and confusion about my role in his ministry to a place of dreaming again about the goodness of God in allowing me to be a part of his work. I again have a passion to serve him. My thirst for knowledge has increased; I am enjoying reading about theology and ministry again! Most importantly to me, my wife and I are working together to actively find our role in serving the kingdom and shepherding his flock!

Debrief

Here was a young man who felt a call of God on his life, had responded to it, and then was deeply wounded by both churches he tried to serve. Unfortunately, he is not the first pastor to receive such treatment from a church, and his experiences made him reluctant to return to a ministry position even though he clearly felt called to do so.

I do not know why some churches harm ministers the way they do, but I do know such treatment of ministers is the reason so many leave the ministry every year. I also know that a number of ministers I have coached have carried a lot of pain, much of which they have never shared with anyone. It's simply not healthy for someone to carry such burdens and have no one to talk to. But I also understand the reluctance of many ministers to share their struggles and challenges with others. Whom will they tell? Most ministers do not want their colleagues to think they are weak or, perhaps, so spiritually immature that they struggle with these issues. They are also unwilling to tell judicatory leaders who may control their opportunities to move to other churches in the future.

These examples and more demonstrate why having a coach is so helpful. Pastor B and I never saw each other in person. I lived some distance from him, belonged to a different denomination, and was completely committed to helping him live his life to the fullest. He was free to tell me anything he wanted without being afraid that it could ever be used to harm him, his family, or his ministry.

Coaches will also have to decide how to handle information that would be impacted by personal beliefs. Pastor B is a good example. Some people would immediately determine that his divorce made him ineligible for future ministry. Such people would have tried to steer the coaching conversations to other things he could do in the church that would not put him in a leadership position. However, that is not the role of a coach.

> A role of a coach is to discover and draw out of persons being coached that which God may be seeking to say to and through them, magnify these discerned truths, point the persons being coached toward action around their discerned truths, and then hold them accountable for effective action.[2]

As a coach, it is not my role to judge a person's past; rather, it is my job to help the individual understand what God is teaching through those previous actions or events. In the case of Pastor B, if a coach strongly felt that a divorced person could not serve in a church leadership position again, he or she should not accept Pastor B as a client. It would not be fair to Pastor B or to the coaching process to impose personal beliefs on the client. At the same time, it was proper to point out the challenges he would encounter as he sought a new church to serve. I reminded him that there would be many churches that would never consider him solely because of the divorce. Without judging him or his sense of call, I wanted to help him realistically understand the challenge he faced.

Another important lesson for coaches is that, any time one works with bivocational ministers, flexibility is key. It frustrated me that it took three sessions before Pastor B met with the other minister, but I understood. Bivocational ministers often struggle trying to match their schedules to someone else's. Coaching appointments often have to be rescheduled, and tasks may not always happen in a timely manner. Knowing this in advance doesn't mean coaches should not keep people accountable to what they say they are going to do, but it does mean that we can extend some grace knowing that time is always going to be a challenge for a bivocational minister.

CHAPTER FIVE

THE BIVOCATIONAL INTERIM PASTOR

Pastor C served one church as a pastor and was, in his opinion, unethically dismissed. The dismissal brought pain to him and his family, resulting in his leaving the ministry for a season and seeking therapy. For the past seven years, he had served as a bivocational interim pastor, a ministry that was mostly enjoyable for him, but his current church at the time we began our coaching relationship was a challenge. His spiritual gifts profile showed his primary gifts to be pastor/shepherding, teaching, and administration, and he scored high on every question of the Life Satisfaction Indicator.

Pastor C seemed intelligent and articulate but also came across as one driven to excellence. He appeared forceful in some of his comments yet understood that he could not force his will upon the church he served. In every session we had, he expressed frustration with his inability to lead his present church in the direction he felt it needed to take.

Session One

In our first session, Pastor C wanted to focus on his frustration with interim ministry in general. He indicated that he normally spent about eighteen months in a church while they sought a new pastor, and then he left for another interim position when the new pastor arrived. He expressed an exhausting feeling of repetition with this type of ministry. He said he would like to stay at one church, to see the fruits of his labor, a desire that caused him to wonder if it was time to consider seeking a more permanent pastoral position.

He admitted that part of his frustration with interim ministry might also result from the lack of success he had seen in his current church. The church was not healthy when he arrived, due to a number of unresolved issues several years in the making. As a result, attendance had declined by about half over the previous decade. Although the church insisted they wanted to return to their previous size, they resisted every suggestion that could help them become a healthier congregation. He was actually told by some church leaders that he was only the interim pastor and would soon be gone. They would wait until they had a new pastor before making any changes. Of course, such an attitude negates much of the reason for having an interim pastor, but the church seemed not to understand that, or else they didn't care.

I spent a major portion of this first session trying to encourage Pastor C. Because of his drive to succeed, his failure to be effective in that church placed a lot of emotional stress on him and probably on his family. He was scheduled to meet with his judicatory leader the following day, and at that meeting he would ask what steps he needed to take to help turn the church around.

Session Two

Pastor C found that the judicatory leader shared many of his same frustrations with his church. Part of the frustration was due to the fact that the judicatory leader did not have a good working relationship with the church and found that they seldom followed his recommendations. This news further discouraged Pastor C and caused him to wonder if anything he did in the church would make a difference.

During this session, the pastor identified one individual who seemed to be behind much of the turmoil in the church. Pastor C had noted that few people were willing to stand up to this controller, allowing her to set the tone for everything that happened. Although he was willing to challenge her, he knew he could not succeed because he would not have the support of the congregation.

As Pastor C continued to complain about his inability to help the church, I challenged him to consider lesser goals than the ones he had achieved at previous churches. I reminded him that each church is different, and perhaps he could still help the church if he set different, less lofty goals and worked to achieve them. This seemed to give him a measure of hope, and he committed to identifying three to six reasonable goals he could achieve in his time with that congregation. Along with each goal, I also asked him to identify one intentional action he would need to take to accomplish the goal.

Session Three

Our third session did not begin well. The pastor's wife had developed some health issues since our previous session. All tests conducted revealed that everything was benign, which they celebrated, but during her illness, some of the church members questioned whether Pastor C would be able to minister adequately to them. He now better understood why the previous two pastors had left the church, and why one of their wives had developed a deep dislike for the church. He himself was hurt by their lack of concern for him and his wife.

Pastor C had, however, completed his assignment and identified five goals with some action steps for each one. Each goal was doable in his current context. One included updating his own personal résumé because he felt it was time for him to return to stationary pastoral ministry. When I asked him the benefits he saw in serving as a stationary pastor, he listed three. However, he also identified three challenges, some of which involved his current inability to move from the immediate area due to family commitments.

I asked Pastor C if he had considered serving as a bivocational pastor. Although he had served as a bivocational interim, he had not considered bivocational ministry as a stationary pastor. He wasn't sure what he could do outside of ministry, so we began to explore that possibility. I reminded him of his giftedness in the area of teaching, and he admitted that he often wondered if that might be something he would enjoy doing. It surprised him to learn that there were opportunities to be an adjunct teacher online as well as other teaching opportunities that would not require him to be tied to a classroom each day. His assignment before our next session was to talk to some teachers he knew to learn more about how to pursue that possibility.

Session Four

Both of the teachers Pastor C knew were gone on vacation, so he was not able to complete his assignment. He said he had left messages for both of them and hoped to talk to them soon.

Pastor C wanted to use our fourth session to discuss the church controller. He had talked to church leadership about their need to include consideration of a bivocational pastor as part of their pastoral search. Due to their shrinking finances he did not believe they could afford to call a fully-funded pastor. Later, in his absence, the controller insisted to the congregation that they should not listen to his advice and should continue to seek a fully-funded pastor, an action that only increased Pastor C's level of frustration with the church as a whole.

Few in the church seemed truly interested in his leadership. He felt stuck there because of his inability to relocate, and there didn't seem to be another church nearby that would be a good fit for him theologically. He knew a confrontation with the controller would not resolve anything because he would have no support from anyone in the congregation. Pastor C did admit that the church moderator seemed supportive of his ministry and had been one person who tried to encourage him during his time there. After further questioning, Pastor C decided to talk to the moderator, and if he was agreeable, the two of them would meet together with the controller.

Session Five

Pastor C and the moderator met with the controller, but nothing was resolved. As expected, no one in the congregation supported the pastor in the encounter, which further discouraged Pastor C, so we discussed how he was taking care of himself. I was pleased to hear he performed several regular routines to maintain some sense of balance in his life.

The topic for session five was how he could help the members of the congregation prepare themselves for the pastoral search process. In the Baptist denomination, interim pastors are usually asked not to involve themselves in the search process, so I asked Pastor C whether it was appropriate for him to be so involved in that discussion. He responded that his judicatory had asked him to be involved, perhaps because of the judicatory leader's inability to establish much of a relationship with the church. He felt the search committee was moving forward without giving much thought to what the church needed in a pastor, what they could afford, and the future of the church. I challenged him to discuss these questions with the judicatory leader and the church moderator and report back.

Session Six

Once again, Pastor C was upset at the start of our session. Although he had talked with the moderator and the committee about the search committee's need to slow down the search process, they refused to listen to his advice. Every church in which he had served as an interim had been a healthier congregation when he left, and he was certain this would not be the case with this church. I have seldom talked with a pastor who felt so negative about his work. In an attempt to encourage him, I asked if he could identify anything positive he had accomplished in his time there. He actually identified three positive changes, and I pointed out that these were significant changes for the better in fewer than two years.

Then I changed the direction of the discussion and asked if his call to this church might not have been for him to help the church become healthier but to help him address some of the issues in his own life. His frustrations with the church had certainly brought a lot of his own perfectionist tendencies and his drive to succeed to the surface. Perhaps this ministry was intended for God to help him work on his issues. Pastor C indicated that he had actually begun wondering that himself over the past few weeks. Although our coaching agreement had come to an end, he promised to continue to work on his issues as well as try to help the church become healthier during his remaining time with them.

Debrief

Most people go into ministry wanting to make a difference in people's lives. Although I've not seen studies on it, I assume many of us are Type A personalities who are driven to succeed. It becomes difficult for us to be in situations in which we cannot see results.

Pastor C, as an interim and bivocational pastor, felt he never had the opportunity to enjoy the fruits of his ministry. He felt trapped in a cycle of starting over with a new church, rebuilding, instilling in them healthy practices, and then allowing the selected stationary pastor to take over. Pastor C saw no way to end the cycle, especially because of his inability to move.

This is not an uncommon problem for many bivocational ministers. One of the advantages of bivocational ministry is the opportunity to develop roots in our communities, but those roots can also limit future ministry opportunities. I have met many pastors unwilling to relocate because their children are about to graduate from high school and they don't want to disrupt their lives, or they are unable (or unwilling) to sell their homes, or their spouses have good jobs and don't want to move, or there are parents nearby who need their assistance, or any number of other reasons that prevent them from moving. Unwillingness or inability to relocate may seriously impact or limit a pastor's ministry options. As the number of churches being served by bivocational ministers continues to increase, so will this problem.

We must help both pastors and churches understand that there is value in long-term ministry and that churches need to look for pastors who want to stay long term. For many churches, this means seeking a bivocational minister who will not be totally dependent on the church to meet the financial needs of his or her family. Problems will arise in any long-term relationship, and the ability to work through those problems will often determine how long the relationship lasts. Just as with marital relationships, it is generally healthier for pastors and churches to work through conflicts together than to end the relationship at the first sign of trouble.

Part of Pastor C's problem, however, was his church's unwillingness to address long-term conflicts. The church members had a poor relationship with their judicatory and were unwilling to work with the individual assigned to the church. It appeared to be a dysfunctional church led by dysfunctional people supported by an apathetic membership. After such churches repeatedly refuse every effort to assist them, it's time to leave them to wander aimlessly in the wilderness. Jesus says not everyone will receive the gospel, and there is a time to shake the dust from one's feet and move on to a place that will receive it (Matthew 10:14). We have sacrificed enough good pastors on the altars of dysfunctional churches.

Pastor C needed encouragement. He had been so frustrated for such a long time that he could no longer see the good results of his ministry. In nearly every session we had, he spoke of his sense of failure, yet he could name positives when prompted. He just needed someone to help him step back and take a balcony view of his ministry. Coaches should be among the most positive and encouraging people around because they have a great opportunity to come alongside and lift the spirits of those who struggle with the various challenges of life and work.

CHAPTER SIX

THE NEW PASTOR

Pastor D spent much of his life as an atheist. As we began our coaching relationship, he had been a Christian for ten years and a pastor for only two. He was in his final year of his denomination's lay-ministry training program. His scores all indicated that he was generally satisfied with his life, was highly task oriented, and a rather poor administrator.

Pastor D frequently missed sessions, and it finally became necessary to confront him about what appeared to be a lack of commitment on his part. He insisted he was committed, however, and I continued our relationship but warned him that if he missed another session without prior notification, the coaching relationship would end.

Session One

Pastor D serves in the only existing church in a small community of about 1,500 people. As we began our first session, he identified three concerns with his church and its ministry in their community. One, a fairly large percentage of people in the community called themselves Christians but did not attend church services. Two, the church had a sizable sum of money that he wanted to use to minister to the community. Third, he himself lived thirty miles from the church and sometimes struggled to be available when needed. After some discussion, Pastor D chose to focus on the first concern.

I asked Pastor D why he thought, in general, many self-proclaimed Christians did not attend church. He named two primary reasons: 1) They have been hurt by the church in the past; 2) Many see the contemporary church as irrelevant. It was obvious that Pastor D had a burden for these individuals and wanted to find ways to reach out to them and draw them back to the church. As we spoke, he mentioned that the leadership of his church was meeting that night, and said he would ask them to help him identify the inactive members of the church and others in the community he could reach out to.

As we neared the end of our time together I asked Pastor D if his church had ever done a Strengths, Weaknesses, Opportunities, and Threats (SWOT) analysis. He did not know if they had but believed there might be value in the church working through such an analysis and said he would approach the leadership team about it. Reporting back on the results of his meeting with the leadership team was his assignment for our next session.

Session Two

As we began this session, Pastor D told me he had led the church's leadership team through a SWOT analysis, which appeared to be a helpful evaluation but revealed that the weaknesses exceeded the strengths of the church. However, they had identified a number of strengths that could be used in offering quality ministry to their community. They also found several opportunities to minister to the community that allowed them to see the church's *potential*. Pastor D was pleased with the results of the study and felt it represented a breakthrough for some on the leadership team.

In our second session, the pastor wanted to focus on what he called his holy discontent. Before becoming a pastor, he spent much of his time talking with unchurched people about their relationship with God. Now he said he spent most of his ministry time with church people and did not have the opportunities to share his faith with others. His employer had also increased his work hours, allowing even less time for ministry. Pastor D's spiritual gifts assessment showed him to have high scores in evangelism, and he was frustrated that he did not have the opportunity to use that gift to lead others to Christ. In addition, he was about to complete his denomination's lay-ministry training. Because of his discontent, he wanted to evaluate his ministry options. As I asked him about those options, he identified four possibilities.

- He could remain bivocational at his present church.
- He could increase his hours at his present church from 15 to 20.
- He could serve two or three yoked churches.
- He could pursue fully-funded ministry.

As we discussed these options he expressed that he felt drawn to the fourth one, which would require him to continue his education (something he enjoyed) and allow him to focus all his energy on one thing. He had a meeting scheduled soon with his judicatory leader and planned to discuss the four options with him and ask for his advice.

Near the end of our session, Pastor D mentioned some ongoing relationship issues with a few persons in the church. A long-time member had resigned her position in the church, and Pastor D was uncertain why. I encouraged him to talk with this individual and to look for ways to rebuild relationships with everyone in the church. In our next session he was to report back on the conversation with the unhappy member as well as the one with his judicatory leader.

Session Three

Our next session did not occur for several weeks due to Pastor D having surgery, which gave him extra time to think about his holy discontent and talk to several people about it. His judicatory leader encouraged him to continue his education at one of the denominational schools and pastor a church in that area while attending classes. His wife suggested they not address the issue until he actually completed his lay-ministry training, and he agreed. He also had time to talk to the unhappy church member and found she had some personal issues with him. They used the discussion to work through their differences, and she returned to the church.

Another leadership meeting had occurred since our last session, and the church leaders made several important ministry decisions. They decided to re-activate their weekly prayer meeting and start a men's Bible study for men not currently involved in a church. It would be a video study held in the home of one of the leaders. The prayer meeting was intended for spiritual growth among the current membership, and the study would be an outreach tool for unchurched persons living in the community.

Pastor D wanted to focus our time in the third session on staffing issues in smaller churches. Like many small churches, Pastor D's church had trouble finding persons for all the positions in the church. As we discussed this problem, the pastor recognized that, like many small churches, they were trying to do too much with their limited resources. He saw the value in eliminating some positions and programs that were no longer effective but also recognized the difficulties he might face in trying to eliminate them. The most pressing need centered around their lack of a regular pianist for their music worship.

Before our next session, Pastor D was to meet with the music worship committee to address the problem and seek possible solutions.

Session Four

There was another extended time before we could meet again because Pastor D developed an infection from his previous surgery and had to have another surgery. The prayer meetings had begun and were going well. The differences that had caused the original pianist to leave the church were resolved, and she returned, solving that problem for the time being.

Pastor D wanted to focus on two issues in our fourth session. It is usually best to focus on only one, but both of these bothered him quite a bit, and I felt we should probably address them.

The first was the formation of the men's Bible study. It was scheduled to meet early on Saturday mornings. His work schedule had been changed, requiring him to work quite late on Saturday nights. His fear was that if he met with the men early on Saturday morning and had to work late on Saturday night, he would not function well on Sunday mornings. His only two options were to see if he could get his work schedule changed or find someone else to lead the men's study.

The second issue was that he thought one of the leader's wives was too involved in church activities. Although she was doing a very good job, Pastor D was afraid she would burn out. He also recognized her involvement as preventing others from being involved in the life of the church. He wanted to talk to her but did not want to offend her. After discussing this for several minutes, Pastor D decided to talk to her husband before speaking to her. He wanted her husband's sense of how she would respond.

Another issue came up during our discussion about the structure of the church Pastor D served. For a church its size, the structure in place no longer made sense. The church did not have a constitution or any document detailing its structure but had recently begun working on one. Pastor D thought this would be a good time to address the church's structure and try to eliminate some positions and boards that were no longer needed.

Prior to our next meeting, Pastor D would talk to the husband of the over-involved woman, and if that went well, he would talk to the woman about delegating some of her responsibilities. He would also talk to his supervisor about changing his work schedule, making his involvement in the men's Bible study more feasible.

Session Five

Because I previously questioned Pastor D's commitment to the coaching process, he kept our regularly scheduled fifth appointment, even though he was on vacation with his family. He reported that the discussion with the church leader had gone well, but the leader cautioned Pastor D not to talk to his wife until he returned from vacation. In the meantime, the leader promised to talk to his wife himself to get her reaction to the pastor's concerns.

In this session, the pastor wanted to focus on an upcoming baptism at his church, which would be the first baptism at the church in fifty years. Everyone was excited, but Pastor D was concerned he would do something to ruin it for everyone. The baptism would take place in a small river that ran through the community. He thought it would attract onlookers, and he didn't want to do anything that would take away from the seriousness of the event.

As we began talking about the baptism, it was obvious Pastor D had given it much thought. As their worship service ended that day, the congregation was going to walk together to the river for the baptism. It would certainly attract attention in their small community.

In addition, the church planned to host a community picnic following the baptism, and that evening, the church would have its first monthly community movie night. This baptism had the potential of not only being a meaningful time for the people being baptized, but it also had great potential for outreach to the community, causing the pastor to feel pressured.

Another concern was that, because the river wasn't very deep, they would have to walk out some distance from the bank to be able to baptize properly. One of the baptismal candidates might stumble and fall into the river. He contemplated the idea of asking some of the church leadership to walk out into the river to assist the candidates as they approached the pastor.

Session Six

Heavy rains almost washed out the plans for the baptism because the river flooded, a turn of events that turned out to be a blessing since they didn't have to go so far out into the river. The baptism was everything Pastor D had dreamed. The church was packed with the friends and families of the persons being baptized, and a number of people from the community came to the river to witness the ceremony. They stayed for the picnic that afternoon, and many returned for the movie that night. The movie was so well attended that the church decided to have one each month.

Pastor D had also been able to speak to his supervisor about his work schedule, which the supervisor then changed, allowing Pastor D to lead the Saturday Bible study. In addition, one man in the community—not a church member—became so excited when he heard about this ministry he volunteered to cook breakfast each morning for those attending.

For our final session Pastor D wanted to talk about a member of the church who had been diagnosed with cancer. This individual was a private person who did not want anyone to know of his illness. The pastor wanted to share it with his prayer team but didn't want to betray confidences. As we explored the options, he decided he would first talk to the individual's wife and then ask the individual for permission to share his illness with others.

As we concluded our time together, he talked about how helpful the coaching relationship had been for him. He had assumed coaching would be like consulting. He expected to present problems and get solutions from me. Pastor D appreciated the coaching process because it allowed him to discover the solutions himself. My questions forced him to think through the issues and find solutions that fit his circumstances.

Debrief

Pastor D balanced numerous responsibilities and commitments, which meant that sometimes he did not give coaching the priority it needed. A key element in coaching is accountability. Coaching clients must do what they say they will do between sessions, or there is little to be gained from a coaching relationship.

Coaching clients also must keep the scheduled appointments. Pastor D called the first time he needed to reschedule, but the next two times, I never heard from him until I sent an email. After the second time, I questioned his commitment to coaching. He did not miss another session after we discussed the importance of keeping the appointments.

Coaches must not be afraid to challenge their clients. Ministers *do* have numerous responsibilities, but that does not mean they should get a free pass on accountability. Emergencies do arise, and allowances must be made, but simply forgetting an appointment because the minister is busy doing something else is not acceptable. Pastors have to set priorities in their scheduling, and if one is to be coached, that has to become a priority and commitment.

As a coach, when I have an appointment with someone, I am at my desk at least thirty minutes before the appointment. If someone misses a call I give him or her fifteen minutes before sending an email. I have scheduled my day around that expected call. Ignoring it or forgetting to reschedule if something comes up demonstrates a lack of respect for my time and commitment to the coaching relationship, and persons who do this more than once must be called out. If the coaching client is not held accountable, the coaching experience loses its value.

One of Pastor D's issues revolved around relationships in the church. Many pastors do not understand the importance of relationships in the small-church setting. In the small church, everything revolves around relationships. Virtually every decision made will depend on how that decision might impact the current relationships that exist in the church. Pastors can be theologically sound and highly skilled and educated, but if they do not work on their relationships with people in the church, their ministries will not be successful. In Pastor D's case, he had two members who had left. Then, after he visited them and spoke to them personally, both of them returned, which is an indication that their grievances were not severe, but they wanted those grievances heard and addressed. My coaching relationship with Pastor D forced him to be accountable to doing things that made him uncomfortable but were ultimately necessary for the health of the church and effectiveness of his ministry.

CHAPTER SEVEN

THE INTENTIONAL BIVOCATIONAL PASTOR

Pastor E was a seminary graduate who served several years as a fully-funded pastor before deciding to become bivocational in 1984. At the time our coaching relationship began, he worked as a teacher and pastored a small church that was about to close its doors when they decided to hire him. Although the church continued to have some struggles, Pastor E believed it was becoming a healthier church and had seen some recent growth.

His highest scores on the Life Satisfaction Indicator were his relationships with his family. His lowest scores were fun and hobbies. Like many bivocational ministers, Pastor E struggled to make time for himself and his interests. He also struggled to say no and often found himself overextended. Because of this trait, we found it difficult to make appointments for our sessions.

Session One

In our first session Pastor E wanted to talk about how soon he would be able to lead the church he served. In the thirty months he had been the pastor, the church had grown from an average of thirteen people to thirty, but the leadership continued to come from the older members, and they were reluctant to share leadership with the pastor or anyone else in the church. The previous pastor's ministry had been divisive and was a major reason the church nearly closed its doors. Pastor E understood the leaders' reluctance but also wanted their trust.

We spent much of our time discussing trust issues and how he could build and gain the congregation's trust. It sounded like he had been doing a lot of the right things, and I encouraged him to continue. He knew it would take time to earn the trust of the congregation and the church leaders, but I discussed with him the concept of learning to lead through the existing leaders. He identified two persons who held most of the authority in the church.

Pastor E then named two changes he would like to make. First, he wanted to use more contemporary music in their services, and second, he wanted to use video equipment. When I asked how he might accomplish that, he said he would first talk to the two primary leaders about his wishes, and if they agreed, he would ask the church board for approval. I affirmed his plans, and he committed to having those conversations before our next coaching session.

Session Two

At the start of our second session, Pastor E reported that the board had agreed to purchase the video system and would probably agree to a new sound system later. The success was even sweeter when they discovered that an accounting error had been made in their financials and the church actually had sufficient money to go ahead with the purchase. Pastor E felt they had taken an important step in the church's ability to move forward.

Pastor E had focused much of his ministry in this church on the youth, which was what he wanted to address in this session. He had little problem getting young people involved in activities in the church, but he was concerned that little spiritual growth occurred. When prompted, Pastor E identified several characteristics he would like to see developed in his youth. I then asked what needed to happen in his youth group to inspire development. He thought many in the youth group needed to be stretched out of their comfort zones, and he had some events planned for later in the year that he believed would accomplish that.

After a short divergence from that topic onto another one, Pastor E circled back to the youth ministry discussion and began to express frustration and disappointment. When I asked him questions about the youth ministry, he admitted there were no young people in the church when he first arrived. He told me the church had spent $4,000 in his first year just on youth ministry, and that the lives of several young people had been changed as a result. I spent our final minutes helping him recall all that had been accomplished with young people in only thirty months, which helped him feel optimistic again about his ministry.

The project he wanted to accomplish before our next session was to develop plans for the church's youth ministry for the remainder of the year.

Session Three

Pastor E reported three goals for the youth as we began our third session. All three met the criteria established in our previous session, so I affirmed his goals. The specifics of the goals are not important to the coach as long as they meet the criteria the coaching client has established.

For this session, Pastor E wanted to address his educational concerns. Pastor E was in his mid-fifties and wanted to retire from teaching before turning sixty. Like many ministers that age, he had been thinking about pursuing a doctorate degree in ministry. He had a master's in religious education, with an additional forty hours beyond. He had been talking to two seminaries about his doctorate and was in the process of submitting paperwork to one of them for evaluation. There were three questions I asked:

- How do you believe additional education will benefit you?
- What are the gaps in your training that you want to correct?
- What do you enjoy about the learning process?

His answers suggested that pursuing a doctorate would be a good option for him, so I encouraged him to do that.

His homework assignment before our next session was to complete the paperwork and send it to the seminary he had chosen and to plan his fall ministry and preaching schedule at the church.

Session Four

Pastor E had written out his preaching schedule and planned part of the fall ministry at the church. There were some issues that had to be worked out before he could finish the ministry plans. Unfortunately, a reference failed to sign his paperwork for the seminary, so Pastor E was unable to complete that part of his assignment.

Our fourth session was difficult because Pastor E did not come prepared to discuss any particular issue. After several prompts, he finally said the church needed to focus more on evangelism, which became the focus of the session. During our discussion it became apparent that he was the one who needed to be more focused on evangelism. Everything he identified as a need was primarily his responsibility as pastor. He decided to preach more messages about evangelism. He believed the church needed some evangelism training then admitted that there were several resources on his desk that could be used for that purpose.

His assignment before our next session was to identify some workshops and other resources that would help the church become more evangelistic.

Session Five

This was a much better session than the previous one due to several activities occurring at the church. A new children's ministry and a new Bible study class were beginning, both of which had Pastor E excited. He had gone through the evangelism materials on his desk and found some that would help him emphasize evangelism in the church later in the year. What had him most excited was that he discovered a conference he could take the youth group to that would help them better understand their sexuality. (In a previous session, Pastor E expressed a concern with a growing trend he had observed of young people identifying themselves as homosexual simply because they didn't fit into any of the other peer-designated categories.)

The issue Pastor E wanted to address in our fifth session was his perfectionism, which led to a difficulty delegating responsibilities to other people. I asked him what might happen if he did not learn to delegate to others, and he answered immediately, an indication he had been thinking about this issue for some time. I then asked him what he needed to do to feel more comfortable in delegation, and he identified four things.

- Spend more time with church members to know them on a deeper personal level.
- Give each member a spiritual gifts assessment to help both himself and the members better understand how God has gifted them.
- Develop a structure to hold people accountable.

• Reward people who do a good job.

His immediate response again reflected that he had spent some time thinking about this prior to our session. I congratulated him on his responses and affirmed them. Once again, a basic tenet of coaching is revealed with this example: People often already know what they need to do; they just need someone to draw that out of them and affirm their decisions.

As we discussed his assignment for our last session, Pastor E stated he wanted to write his assessment of the church and discuss it with church leaders. Included in that assessment would be his view of his ministry with the church to date and his vision for the church.

Session Six

Unfortunately Pastor E had not completed his final assignment due to increased work demands. While accountability is important, good coaches know when to exercise flexibility because of the time constraints all pastors (but especially bivocational pastors) must balance. Since this was our last session, there was little I could do, so it seemed best not to dwell on the topic.

Pastor E wanted to focus on the church's ministry to young families. Though the church had a few such families, they were largely not involved in church activities. Pastor E figured most of them believed that giving the church one hour a week was sufficient. He was also concerned about the lack of spiritual growth he saw in many of these family members.

One of the questions I asked was what these families had in common. Pastor E noted that many of them were interested in sports, and he immediately mentioned that he thought they might enjoy a father-son trip to the local, minor-league baseball park. He also thought cookouts would be a good way to connect these families to the church.

Debrief

Pastor E enjoyed a productive ministry in his church, but his view of his own ministry was different because things didn't happen as quickly as they had in previous churches he'd been in, and he felt that he was somehow responsible. He struggled to see the positive things because he frequently focused on areas in which he came up short. Pastor E simply needed the same thing so many other bivocational pastors need: encouragement, and help stepping back and looking at the big picture of his overall ministry in his church.

Pastor E also represented a learning opportunity for me as a coach when he became the first person to come to one of the coaching sessions without any idea what to discuss. We spent about twenty minutes of our hour trying to get him to identify one thing we could discuss. It was a terrible waste of our time and reflected poor preparation from both of us. From that session, I learned that some basic preparation on my part could help combat the feeling that we are just wasting our time. Good coaches should have key inquiry questions ready to ask in the event that a coaching client attends a session needing some guidance or direction about what to discuss.

In his post-coaching assessment, Pastor E mentioned an appreciation for the focused and intentional structure of our sessions and the attention given to the time limit. Everyone is busy, and it is important for coaches to honor the time and the commitment of the people they coach, especially if they are bivocational ministers, who—more likely than not—have squeezed the slot for their coaching sessions into packed schedules already bookended by other commitments.

CHAPTER EIGHT

THE DIFFICULT CHURCH

Pastor F was a pastor I know personally who served a church I also knew. Such situations can be challenging to the coach because the temptation is always there to allow your prejudices and prior knowledge to impact your coaching. Coaches must be careful not to switch from a coaching model to a consulting role in these situations.

Pastor F began his ministry with a college education but no theological training. He had been active as a lay leader in his home church and felt called to bivocational ministry. His pastor strongly supported his call to ministry and led his church to license him.

He scored high in every category on his Life Satisfaction Indicator. His lowest score was in his relationships with parishioners, and I knew this was likely more the fault of the church than of Pastor F. The church membership was rather cold, with a history of rapid pastoral turnover. Pastor F's original goal for the church was to lead it to a place where it would be similar to the one he had previously served as a lay leader: forward thinking and eager to take the gospel to the community. The reason he sought a coaching relationship was that he soon became frustrated with the maintenance mindset that existed in this church, and he wanted some guidance in exploring his options.

Session One

Pastor F soon realized that introducing any change into this church would be a challenge. Although the people seemed to enjoy his preaching and ministry, they highly resisted any changes he proposed, even the small ones. He wanted to introduce a more contemporary musical worship style in an effort to attract young people, but he soon realized that would not be approved. Pastor F was frustrated by the stubbornness he encountered because the search committee had said that one of the things they wanted in their next pastor was someone who could reach young families, yet his every effort created conflict. We began to explore smaller changes he might be able to make with the belief that, as the church made minor changes, it would become more comfortable with the idea of change in general, which might allow him to introduced major changes in the future.

He identified two minor changes he believed might be acceptable to the congregation. One was to move the piano to a different location on the platform. The second was to improve the church sign. It had long needed to be repainted and updated. Pastor F thought these were two changes most people would agree to make. His assignment before our next meeting was to talk to the church leaders about them.

Session Two

Pastor F reported that both changes were agreed to by the church leaders and congregation. Even though they were minor changes, he thought it was a step in the right direction.

In our second session, he wanted to address the dearth of young adult membership. Pastor F's church was located in a sparsely populated rural area. Most growth would have to come from people willing to drive some distance. In the few months he had been at the church, two young couples had begun attending services there. After I asked some questions, Pastor F determined that the best way to attract more young adults might be through these new couples. He resolved to meet with them to determine what had attracted them to the church and what would make the church more appealing to their friends. His meeting with them was to occur before our next session.

Session Three

In our time apart, Pastor F learned that he and his wife were the primary reasons the two young couples began attending his church. The two couples were agreeable to inviting their friends to church, but all parties recognized that the church did not have much to offer young couples. As a result, Pastor F had decided this obstacle would be the agenda for discussion for this session.

The Sunday school program in Pastor F's church was limited to a handful of people, most of whom had attended the same class for years. Pastor F believed it would be important to create new Sunday school classes for young adults and children who might come into the church. These classes would not only provide discipleship training but would also offer fellowship activities for the new people, something they would not receive in the existing classes.

Pastor F set a goal of offering these new classes within the next two months. I then began to question him about what needed to happen to be prepared to offer these classes so quickly. He recognized that acquiring teachers was the first priority he would have to address. Although he was willing to teach the adult class, he would have to find volunteers to teach the children's class, and he wasn't sure there would be people qualified to do that who did not already teach. Leadership development had not been a high priority in this church for a number of years. The same people had kept the same responsibilities for years, and new people had not been developed or encouraged to assume any roles in the church. His task before our next session would be to obtain permission from the church to start new classes and to try to identify qualified people to teach the new children's class.

Session Four

The church approved the start of the new Sunday school classes, and Pastor F found someone to teach the children's class. The church sign had been painted since the start of our coaching relationship, and the church had agreed to host an upcoming association meeting. Pastor F felt much better about his ministry there, and wanted to spend our fourth session discussing how he might praise the church congregation for their willingness to try new things and to encourage them to continue. He had already thought through some things he would do, I spent much of the session simply affirming his suggestions and ideas. He would report back at our next session about how the people responded to his praise and encouragement.

Session Five

As expected, the church responded well to Pastor F's praise. His adult Sunday school class had begun with only the two new couples attending, but they had already decided on a class event to which they would invite their friends.

For the fifth session, Pastor F wanted to examine how he might develop leaders within the church. The church had only three deacons, all of whom had served for a number of years, and none of whom had ever received much training as deacons.

Even though Pastor F had been a deacon in his previous church, he was uncertain what specific areas of training his deacons might want. He knew some areas in which they *needed* training but wasn't sure they would accept it. He decided to ask them to identify specific areas of training they would like to receive.

Pastor F also believed that potential new leaders needed to be identified and trained. Leadership responsibilities had remained in the hands of a select few people for several years, resulting in the church's stagnation. Pastor F rightly believed that new leaders needed to be developed and allowed to assume positions of leadership in order to initiate new ideas and methods of execution.

The assignment before our next session was for Pastor F to talk to the existing deacons about training they would like to receive and to try to identify some potential new leaders within the congregation.

Session Six

Pastor F was somewhat frustrated as our last session began because his deacons could not identify any areas of training they needed. The pastor couldn't think of any area in which they *didn't* need training, but he also understood that they resisted even the suggestion that they might need training. Because training had been neglected for so long in the church, there were no new people ready to step into leadership positions, and few people he could identify who would be ready soon for a leadership position.

Despite his frustration with this realization, Pastor F had promised the church when they interviewed him that he would stay there at least two years, so he was committed to a minimum of one more year. For our final session, he wanted to focus on his vision for the upcoming year. He believed the growth of the new adult Sunday school class was essential for both his goals of growing the church and developing new leaders. He also wanted to return to his original goal of introducing contemporary music.

Pastor F was prepared for most of the questions I asked about each of his goals and seemed to have thought through them well. I affirmed his goals as challenging but certainly worthy, and concluded our time by affirming him personally and his ministry at the church. He had gone into a difficult place and made some good strides forward. I encouraged him to resist frustration with any slow progress he would undoubtedly experience because he was challenging the church as it had not been challenged in several years.

Postscript

Because of my personal relationship with both the pastor and the church, I know how his plans and ministry there ended. He gave them the additional year he had promised but was unable to accomplish his goals. Although the church agreed to some of his suggestions, they only went so far until they strongly resisted any further changes. Following Pastor F, they had a series of short-term pastors, each resulting in further conflicts and loss of members. The new people who had joined the church left soon as Pastor F left, and the church returned to its core group of members who had long ago accepted one another's dysfunctional behavior. Despite his frustration with that specific church, Pastor F did not abandon the ministry altogether but accepted another bivocational pastorate and enrolled in a distance-learning program to earn a theological degree.

Debrief

There are no guarantees that coaching will produce the results you might prefer. There are many factors that influence the measure of success that might come from coaching, from the willingness of the person being coached to the receptiveness of the organization to be changed. Pastor F tried to bring change to a dysfunctional church without first bringing some measure of health to the church. It would have been more helpful to him if I had encouraged him to think first about how to lead the church to a healthier place before trying to implement change. In every coaching relationship, the coach should learn just as much as the person being coached, and this was my lesson from this relationship.

At the same time, Pastor F learned some valuable lessons about how to introduce change into a church. He went there with big plans that the church was not ready to receive. As he backed off and introduce smaller changes, he found the congregation more receptive. Every bivocational pastor needs to learn this lesson. Even if you have big goals for your church, break them down into more manageable pieces and only introduce them one at a time. People are much more agreeable to gradual change than sudden change. Even so, as Pastor F learned, there is no guarantee the church will ever agree to all of the change you want to bring about.

Pastor F went into a highly dysfunctional church, stayed two years, and left frustrated by his inability to minister in that environment. The good news is that his experience did not run him out of the ministry. Unfortunately, this is not always the case. I doubt anyone will ever know how many good, God-called, bivocational ministers have abandoned the ministry because of horrendous experiences in their first churches.

Outside of coaching, judicatory leaders can address this problem by refusing to assist highly dysfunctional churches as they search for new pastors until they take specific steps to overcome their dysfunctions. Judicatory leaders would certainly do well to offer assistance in becoming healthier, but they would be justified in refusing to help in any other way until the churches make steady, noticeable progress toward health.

CHAPTER NINE

THE DISORGANIZED PASTOR

Before we begin with Pastor G, it should be noted that Pastor G and the upcoming Pastor H are both women. Although coaches should be able to put aside their personal beliefs when coaching, this is one situation in which I suggest that, if your personal theological beliefs exclude women from pastoral ministry, no attempt should be made to coach a female minister. It would be difficult to be objective, and the temptation would be great to seize upon any problem the female minister may present as evidence that she was never called to the ministry. Pastors G and H both had challenges, but they were no different from problems that many male pastors have presented.

Pastor G struggled with a number of issues when we began our coaching relationship. Some she identified in her questionnaire involved time management, relationships, self-care, and finances. Her current place of ministry was a difficult one that intensified all the other issues.

Session One

Pastor G had difficulty deciding which issue she wanted to focus on in our first session but finally pinpointed time management as the one that impacted all the other issues, so that was where we began. The problems she had at church demanded more time than she had to give. In addition, she had little help from members of the church. Like too many bivocational pastors, Pastor G was responsible for planning the worship service, preparing the bulletin, attending all committee and board meetings, and leading the outreach efforts. Basically, anything done in the church was the direct result of her efforts. One of her concerns was that she had been neglecting some of her responsibilities at her other job. She feared losing that job because of the amount of time she gave to the church. Another concern was the limited amount of time she gave her family.

When asked, Pastor G could name a number of responsibilities she would like to delegate to others in the church, but she did not know who would accept them. One of the reasons she had so much responsibility was that others had failed to come through in the past. I encouraged her to identify the things she needed to do in the church, at her job, and with her family, and to prioritize them. She agreed to do that before our next session.

Session Two

Pastor G missed a couple of appointments for our second session. She never called to let me know she would be unable to keep the appointments, nor did she have a better reason for it than that she simply forgot. As our second session finally began, we discussed her responsibility to keep appointments, and I reminded her that I was busy too. As with Pastor D, I told her we would end the coaching relationship right then if it was not a priority for her. She insisted that she wanted to continue and promised to call if she was unable to keep a future appointment.

From her comments, it seemed it was not uncommon for her to miss appointments due to her lack of time management. Even though several weeks had passed since our first appointment, she still had not set priorities for her time, a revelation that led to another discussion about the necessity for her to complete assignments. I used this as an opportunity to demonstrate how out of control a person's life can become without prioritization. Without a plan, life can get chaotic, and it becomes easy not to do the things that are most important. Although this was not a pleasant coaching call for either Pastor G or myself, I hoped she had begun to see the need to gain some measure of control over how she used her time. I ended the session by assigning her the same task as before, and she promised to set some priorities for her time.

Session Three

As we began our third session, Pastor G shared some of the priorities she had identified for herself. It was obvious she had worked on the assignment, and even though she still had a long way to go, it was a good start.

The concern she wanted to address in our session was the decline in church attendance and in financial giving. She said she was considering starting a community Bible study, which she believed would give people an opportunity to become acquainted with the church at something less formal than Sunday morning. Her hope was that people who began attending the Bible study might eventually begin attending Sunday services as well. Her plan was to use the Bible study to reach out to the community and help people better understand the Bible. I affirmed the idea with the qualification that it should not further complicate her time-management issues. Pastor G believed she would get help from others and wanted to move forward. We spent the remainder of the session discussing how to implement her plans.

Pastor G believed two things had to happen first. One, church leaders would have to agree to a community Bible study and agree to assist her in making it happen. The second challenge she saw was how to promote it in their small community. I asked her about the various types of promotion she thought might be effective. Although she identified several possible ways to promote it, she believed direct mail might be the most effective. Her tasks before our next session were to talk to her church leaders about her plan and have them approve it and to look into the cost of direct mail.

Session Four

Pastor G was excited that the church leaders had endorsed the Bible study she wanted to begin, and they also had agreed to help. However, she was no longer certain direct mail would be the best way to promote the Bible study and needed to look at other marketing options.

Since our last session, she had experienced some health issues, for which her doctor had recommended an exercise program and diet. In her pre-coaching questionnaire, she had identified a great need in her life for exercise and weight loss, but because of the many demands on her time, she had neglected both.

Pastor G had struggled with weight issues for a number of years. Like many people, she had tried a number of diets, which were effective for a while, but she soon got tired of them and reverted to her poor eating habits. She had also begun a number of exercise routines over the years but had never stayed with them. She recognized that in her effort to do everything else, she had neglected herself. Pastor G was willing to start again with dieting and exercise but was concerned she wouldn't be any more faithful to it than before. I asked her what could she do differently this time that she had not done in her previous attempts. She thought having an accountability partner would be the most helpful, so her assignment for our next session was to begin an exercise program and find an accountability partner.

Session Five

Our fifth session was not very productive because it was difficult to keep Pastor G focused on what we needed to accomplish. She had started her exercise program but had not found an accountability partner. She was already frustrated with having to exercise and watch what she ate, and she knew that if she didn't work on maintaining a positive attitude, she would probably not have more success this time than she'd had in previous attempts to lose weight.

Pastor G was excited that the Bible study was going well, however. The study consisted of basic Bible teachings, which did not demand a great deal of preparation on her part, and which she felt was appropriate for the people she wanted to reach.

No matter what I tried to do, I was unable to get her to focus on any specific issue to address in this session. It seemed she just needed to talk about a lot of different things, which I finally allowed her to do. As we ended our time I reminded her that our next session was our last and that she needed to decide ahead of time what issue she would like to address. Her assignment was to continue her exercise routine and work on maintaining a positive attitude.

Session Six

As we began our final session, Pastor G wanted to share six goals she had developed as part of the priorities she started working on after our first session.

- She wanted to move to a church where she could be fully fund-ed or to one where she could stay bivocational but receive better pay and benefits. Such a transition would help ease some of the financial challenges her family faced.
- She wanted to maintain the exercise program she had started.
- She wanted to create more time for Sabbath in her life.
- She wanted to remain involved in a community-wide spiritual de-velopment group in which she had been involved for several years.
- She wanted to write children's books.
- She wanted to begin speaking to women's groups.

It was easy for me to affirm these goals for her life and minis-try, and my affirmation seemed to encourage her. At the same time, I had to point out that the new activities she listed would require time, which was already a problem for her. We spent our final minutes dis-cussing the challenges she believed she would face as she began to work on her goals.

Debrief

The problem Pastor G had (and many bivocational ministers have this same problem) was that she was so used to living a hectic life-style, she didn't know anything else. It would've been a major chal-lenge for her to stop doing any of the numerous tasks she'd identified as her primary responsibilities. Like many of us, Pastor G had become used to living on adrenaline, which can become addictive. The prob-lem is that, one day, all the energy that allowed you to continue to push yourself past proper limits will vanish and often be replaced by depression or other health issues.

Pastor G was one of the early ministers I coached. I'm not sure she was a good candidate for coaching, although she certainly needed it. Her commitment to the coaching relationship wasn't very good, evidenced by her missing appointments and failure to complete assignments. I doubt she gained much value from our coaching relationship. Since coaching Pastor G, I have tried to determine whether subsequent coaching candidates were able to commit to the time requirements involved with the relationship before agreeing to begin.

Pastor G had a passion for ministry and a clear sense of God's call on her life, but her inability to manage her time affected her ministry negatively. The pastorate she had during our coaching relationship did not end well, and she eventually felt forced to resign. Bivocational ministers must learn to balance their lives and ministries. They need to learn the old business adage of, *Under-promise and over-deliver.* Until bivocational ministers learn how to balance their priorities, they will struggle in every area of their lives, and their ministries will be less effective and less enjoyable than they could be.

CHAPTER TEN

THE PASTORAL PASTOR

Pastor H serves a small church in a small community. In her questionnaire it was obvious she had a great heart for her congregation and for the people who lived in the community, but she didn't think she was the pastor she wanted to be. She doubted her ability to provide the kind of leadership the church needed. She wanted to see more spiritual growth in the members of the church, and she wanted to see the church grow in number, but she wasn't sure what she needed to do to help that happen.

Session One

Pastor H's church was focused inward. They did very little community outreach or ministry. Pastor H wanted to move the church from this maintenance mindset to a missional mindset. When I asked her to name the one thing she would do if she could do anything in ministry, she immediately responded that she had long wished she could lead a ministry for people who had been hurt by the church. I told her that if she were able to develop such a ministry, she would probably not pastor a small church for very long because there are many people in every community who have been hurt by the church.

Pastor H was familiar with a young couple who had been involved in a church until something happened that caused them to leave. She had been developing a relationship with them and wanted to begin some type of Bible study with them. Her assignment before our next session was to see if they would be willing to meet with her for a Bible study, and she would continue to work on developing her dream ministry.

Session Two

Pastor H had met once with the couple and asked if they would be interested in starting a small group Bible study. Although they expressed some initial interest, the pastor had been unable to meet with them again due to the husband's health issues. She informed me she would continue to stay in contact with them.

For our second session, Pastor H wanted to discuss people not attending planned events. Her small church could not hold many events, but even the ones they did schedule were often poorly attended by members of the congregation, which may have driven some of her concerns about her leadership qualifications. Through a series of questions and responses, Pastor H decided the best way to address her concern was to lead the board in doing more intentional planning for their next event. Before scheduling another event, they needed to feel confident that it would be something that would appeal to people, that it did not conflict with other activities in the community, and that the event would be quality and done with excellence.

As we neared the end of our conversation, Pastor H mentioned that another challenge was finding someone in her congregation to help with the children's ministry. Prior to our next session, Pastor H committed to asking a person to lead the children's ministry and to talking with the church leadership about how to improve the quality of their events. She would also try to make another contact with the couple for the Bible study.

Session Three

When the third session began, I learned that Pastor H had completed all her assignments, although it was too early to tell how successful she had been. She had discussed with church leadership her desire for events to be well planned, and they agreed to make an effort when planning the next event. The Bible study was still on hold due to the individual's illness. She had spoken with someone about leading the children's ministry, but the person had not yet decided to do so.

Pastor H had been a member of the church for some time before becoming its pastor. This is not uncommon for many bivocational ministers, but she shared a problem that many experience in such situations. For most of her pastorate she felt that people saw her as a friend who happened to be the pastor. She reported that she felt she had recently turned the corner and people now saw her as the pastor who was also a friend. She felt this was a significant change in attitude and would give her increased liberty to lead the church. I certainly concurred with her assessment.

Her desire for the church was that it move closer to God and, at the same time, become more outwardly focused on the community. As is true in many small churches, there had been little intentional discipleship in the church and little interest in developing a vision for ministry. Pastor H wanted to see both happen, and she realized it needed to begin with her. She rightly understood that she could not lead the church in discerning God's vision if she was not clear about her own vision. She also understood that she needed to grow as a disciple of Christ before she could lead others in such growth.

When I asked her what she saw as her next step, she said she believed she needed to take a private retreat to pray for the church and to sort out what she needed to do. Her assignment for our next session was either to take a personal retreat or schedule a time to do so.

Session Four

I was surprised when Pastor H reported she had taken a personal retreat of a couple of days. I had doubted she would be able to fit in her retreat in the two weeks between our sessions, but she had already demonstrated that she was highly motivated to develop as a pastor and had consistently done everything she committed to. We spent much of our fourth session discussing her retreat and the issues she had determined were keys to the future growth of the church.

She had not abandoned her desire to create a ministry for persons previously wounded by the church, but she had broadened her vision of outreach into the community. She wanted to schedule events that would appeal not only to church members but also to the general population. These would not necessarily be religious or spiritual in nature, but they would draw people to the church and give them an opportunity to see that the church was interested in them as individuals. When asked what types of events she had in mind, she responded that the church could offer a community picnic, have a movie night in the church parking lot, and other similar activities that would not be expensive but have wide appeal to the community.

During her retreat she realized that, like many pastors, she had not really done much to intentionally equip and challenge people for ministry. She felt that most people in her congregation did not understand they had been called to minister and gifted to do so, and she doubted that most of them could identify their spiritual gifts. She decided it would be helpful to do a spiritual gift assessment of everyone in the congregation. She could then challenge them to consider how they might use their gifts for ministry. Pastor H was especially interested in finding out if someone had gifts of evangelism who could lead that effort in the church.

Pastor H also realized that a one-time retreat would not be enough for her spiritual development. As a female pastor in a small-town and country church, she needed someone to talk to. As we explored the possibilities, she decided to approach another female pastor serving nearby in a different denomination. Perhaps she felt as isolated as Pastor H did and would welcome someone to meet with on a regular basis and serve as spiritual mentors to each other.

It was exciting to see the changes that had occurred in Pastor H after only four coaching sessions. She began our relationship feeling uncertain about her effectiveness as a pastor. She had dreams for the ministry of the church that she had never shared with anyone, fearing others would think they were inappropriate. She felt her ministry lacked purpose and direction. In our first session, her voice projected a lot of discouragement and doubt. By the fourth session, she was excited about her ministry and the future opportunities that existed in the church she served. Her voice had become hopeful and much more positive.

Her assignments before our next session were to talk to the leadership about doing a spiritual gift assessment of each member and to contact the other female pastor to see if there was an interest in meeting. She would also begin to assess whether there were persons in the church who could lead the evangelism efforts she wanted for the church.

Session Five

Pastor H began this session with the same excitement she had as we ended our last session. The church leadership had agreed to the spiritual gifts assessment, and the congregation had agreed to take it. She wasn't sure where to obtain an assessment, so I gave her the names of a couple of organizations who had good assessments. The other female pastor had agreed to meet with her, and, depending on how that meeting went, they would schedule regular times to come together as ministry colleagues.

For this session, Pastor H wanted to discuss her sermons. She felt they needed improvement but was uncertain what she needed to do. Pastor H had not had any classes on sermon preparation and delivery; she was doing what had been modeled for her by her previous pastors, but she wasn't sure her sermons were quality. After I asked a few questions, Pastor H decided that part of her meeting with the other pastor might be spent collaborating on sermons.

She asked if she could send me a copy of one of her sermons for my review. I agreed but reminded her that reading a sermon is much different from hearing one. She decided the best option was to send a sermon for me to review and also deliver a fifteen-minute excerpt from the message at our next session. As we ended our time together, I encouraged Pastor H to think about what she wanted to address in what would be our sixth and final session.

Session Six

The sermon Pastor H sent me was very good, and her delivery of it over the telephone was excellent. I did point out to her that hearing a sermon over the phone was still not the best way to judge the quality of someone's delivery, but the content itself was quality. I assured her that, while one can always improve in any area of responsibility, she did not need to worry about the content of her sermons if this was an indication of what she did each week.

For this final session, I replaced my coaching hat for a few minutes with a mentoring hat by suggesting some sermon preparation books she could read and recommending she find someone who could videotape her doing a few sermons. She could review those to identify potential areas of improvement.

Pastor H spent most of our final session expressing how much the coaching sessions had changed her. Our sessions were held during the summer months, which were normally a down time in her church. She said attendance had remained strong that summer, which she believed was in part due to the enthusiasm and optimism she carried from the coaching sessions into her ministry.

Debrief

Unlike some ministers I've coached, Pastor H was highly motivated to improve and to gain as much as possible from the coaching experience. She never missed an appointment. She completed every assignment on time. She remained focused throughout the coaching relationship. The result of her ambition was an amazing change in her attitude and her confidence in her ministry abilities. She became more confident in herself and in the calling God placed on her life. She was already providing her church with quality ministry; she just didn't realize it.

Many bivocational ministers feel isolated in their work. Their second job and the way some people view bivocational ministry often make it difficult for them to develop relationships with other ministers or judicatory leaders. Pastor H felt such isolation. The coaching relationship Pastor H and I had provided her with her first real opportunity to receive the kind of support and encouragement she needed.

People like Pastor H are more likely to develop as ministers through a coaching relationship than they are from attending workshops or conferences. She really didn't need more information. She needed affirmation and someone who could help her bring to the surface the things she already knew to do. Such people are a joy to coach and well worth the investment of time coaching requires.

CHAPTER ELEVEN

THE TRANSITIONAL PASTOR

Pastor I was a fully-funded pastor who needed to transition to bivocational ministry. With a growing family, Pastor I's finances were stretched to the limit. Their home was too small, creating a large amount of stress. His Life Satisfaction Indicator scores were lowest in the areas of friends/social life, fun/hobbies, and physical health. He had served his present church for a number of years, but it had obviously taken its toll on him and his family.

Session One

The stress Pastor I felt was evident in our first meeting. In addition to the aforementioned issues, a small group of people in the church had started personally attacking the pastor's family, driving a wedge between Pastor I and his wife and an even greater wedge between his wife and the church. In fact, she seldom attended services any more. I asked Pastor I what the church leaders were doing to address the issue; he answered that they were mostly ignoring the things being said. They had expressed their belief that the accusations and rumors were not true and evidently believed that was sufficient. Pastor I recognized that he needed to encourage those leaders to become more proactive on his and his wife's behalf, and he decided to ask them to confront the ones making the attacks. Talking to the church leaders was his assignment for our next session.

I then asked Pastor I what he and his wife were doing to resolve the problem. Fortunately, both had recognized the impact it was having on their relationship, and they had started seeing a counselor. I affirmed this as a positive decision each of them had made and encouraged them to continue counseling.

Session Two

Pastor I's discussion with the church leaders resulted in an unexpected decision. During that discussion, Pastor I admitted to the leaders some of the problems he and his family were having. Their finances were tight. Their home—the church parsonage—was too small for their family. These two issues plus the personal attacks from members of the church had created huge problems in his family. The church leaders recognized that each of his concerns was valid but also admitted the church could not afford to provide him with a salary increase. They suggested he consider becoming bivocational, and they would restructure his salary package to include a housing allowance so he could purchase a larger home for his family. The church had been marginally fully funded for several years, and these individuals recognized that they could not continue to ask their pastors to continue working for the salary they could afford. Even though nothing had physically changed, the knowledge that positive changes were coming lifted the spirits of both Pastor I and his wife, and also reconfirmed the support the church leaders and the majority of the church had for them.

Pastor I recognized that there would need to be some changes in the church if he became a bivocational pastor. The church had never had any kind of manual with job descriptions and policies. Pastor I believed now would be a good time for them to develop one. At the same time, the church had been considering rewriting its constitution, and it made sense to Pastor I that the manual should be developed at the same time, and that both should happen while the church made its transition to a different ministry style.

It had also been some time since Pastor I had been employed outside of a church setting. He would need to update his résumé and begin searching for jobs that would fit in with his ministry. He had already identified two positions in the local area that would be a match for his gifts and interests, and both were flexible enough that they would not interfere with his pastoral responsibilities.

Prior to our next meeting, Pastor I would talk to the church leadership about developing a manual and starting work on revising its constitution. He would also apply for the two positions he found.

Session Three

The church council agreed to begin work on revising the church constitution and developing a church manual. Pastor I had sent applications to the two organizations with the open positions. He also reported that, since our coaching sessions had started, he and his wife had had two positive sessions with a pastoral counselor and had made good progress addressing their family issues. From those sessions he realized he needed to make more time for his family, and he wanted to address that concern in this, our third, coaching session.

As I asked him to think about the types of activities his family members enjoyed and could afford, Pastor I began to identify several possibilities. He and his wife had not enjoyed a regular date night since their children had been born, and he felt that was an important place to begin. He also talked about how much he and his boys enjoyed camping. As we neared the end of our session he decided he would take the boys on an overnight camping trip. We discussed some possible date ideas, and he decided to take his wife to an upcoming play in which she had expressed some interest. Both the date and the camping experience were to be completed before our next session.

Session Four

Pastor I and his boys had an enjoyable camping experience, and his wife enjoyed their date. Pastor I committed to continuing such family-centered activities. For this session Pastor I wanted to discuss a number of issues within the church.

One issue was the difficulty the church had receiving timely information from the treasurer. The treasurer no longer attended all the church business meetings, and sometimes when he was there, he had no prepared report to distribute or discuss, which made it difficult for the church to know exactly where it stood financially. Although the pastor did not think this indicated any wrongdoing on the part of the treasurer, he did find such behavior frustrating and thought it was somewhat of a challenge to his leadership. The treasurer had seemingly adopted the idea that he was in control of the church's finances and did not need to report to others. In response to some of my questions, Pastor I decided to talk directly to the treasurer and, if that did not resolve the issue, discuss it with church leadership. If necessary, the church council might need to take steps to remove the treasurer from his position if his behavior did not change.

The second issue Pastor I wanted to discuss had to do with the lack of growth in the church. Although his rural church was on a major highway in its county and had a decent population to draw from, attendance had been stagnant for years. Pastor I believed part of the problem was the lack of a church nursery and a limited children's ministry. The church had a nursery, but it was not staffed. Parents who took their children to the nursery were expected to remain with them. Although church members might understand and be agreeable to that expectation, it was not a viable option for guests.

For years the church had enjoyed a solid youth program but offered little for children. Pastor I thought they needed to be doing more with the children rather than simply waiting for them to become old enough to join the youth group. The church had a few families with young children, and the pastor decided he should talk to them about how to structure a ministry that would appeal to their children. He thought a children's ministry program would also appeal to young children from unchurched families in their community and provide the church with an opportunity to reach out to those families.

Pastor I had several assignments before our next session. One was to follow his plan regarding the treasurer's actions. Another was to address the nursery issue with the church council and the parents of small children. He was hopeful the church could develop a volunteer list from these parents so someone would be in the nursery each week to watch all the children who came. The third assignment was to meet with parents to discuss a children's ministry. He did mention that it might not be possible to have that meeting until after our next session.

Sessions Five and Six

Unfortunately, I did not keep good notes on the last two sessions, so I have to report on them from memory. It is important to make notes of each counseling session immediately after the session. One never knows when it will be necessary to refer back to those sessions.

I seem to remember Pastor I's church treasurer committing to providing reports at each business meeting of the church, and people also volunteered to lead the children's ministry. I don't remember what, if anything, was resolved about the nursery.

The one thing I do remember about these sessions is that our focus for each was the nature of bivocational ministry. Pastor I had never served as a bivocational pastor. He had been contacted by each organization to which he had applied, and interviews were scheduled. He thought it was likely he would be offered one of the two positions, and if that happened, he wanted to know how it would impact his ministry.

Although I continued to function as a coach during these sessions by asking questions and trying to pull out Pastor I's thoughts, I also spent a good amount of time consulting and mentoring. We talked about my experience serving as a bivocational pastor of a church for twenty years. Pastor I probably asked more questions during these sessions than I did, especially about how to handle certain things that might come up in the church. He was also concerned about how his dual role would impact his improving relationships with his family.

As we ended our final session, it was obvious that the coaching had been helpful for Pastor I. He expressed that he felt refreshed and more hopeful about ministry than he had in a long time.

Debrief

As a coach, I tend to be reluctant to switch hats and become more of a mentor or consultant, but in Pastor I's situation, I had to do that in our final two sessions. Since he had never been a bivocational minister, he was concerned about how his ministry would change. His pastoral studies prepared him to serve as a fully-funded pastor, and he wasn't sure how that differed from bivocational ministry. For him to successfully transition from a fully-funded pastorate to a bivocational one, he needed someone who had served as a bivocational minister to help him understand how his ministry would change.

I am convinced we will see many ministers in Pastor I's situation in the coming years. Marginal fully-funded churches will find they can no longer meet the financial requirements of their pastors, and those pastors will need to transition to bivocational ministry. Some will struggle to make that transition and will move to other churches. Other pastors, like Pastor I, will find it is a better fit and will learn to adapt. In such a transition, there will be a learning curve for both the pastor and the church, a curve that can be navigated with good coaching.

I have been able to remain in some contact with Pastor I since our coaching relationship, and I'm happy to report that he was offered one of the jobs he applied for and continues to work at that job today. He also continues to serve the same church, and both he and the church made a successful transition to bivocational ministry.

CHAPTER TWELVE
THE ABANDONED PASTOR

Pastor J scored high on every aspect of his Life Satisfaction Indicator except for fun/hobbies and his satisfaction with ministry. He had served bivocationally for about five years when we first began our coaching relationship and was frustrated with the lack of growth in the church and even more frustrated that no one else in the church was bothered by it. He had been a bivocational pastor for thirteen years and was committed to that ministry, but this was the first church he had pastored that had not grown and showed little interest in growing. He admitted he had a low tolerance for bench warmers and persons who refused to get involved in the ministry of the church.

Like many others I've coached, Pastor J was also frustrated by the lack of time he had to spend with his wife and family. His other job was a day shift, and she worked second shift. They tried to get away on Saturdays, but it seemed to get later each week when they could leave. After some discussion, Pastor J decided to focus on the balance he wanted in his life, especially to find more time to spend with his wife.

Session One

Pastor J clearly understood the importance of maintaining balance in his life; he just wasn't sure how to achieve that balance. He had left a good bivocational pastorate in another state to come to his present position so he could attend seminary. The issue of balance had not been a problem in his previous churches, but now it seemed like an uphill battle. He understood that a significant part of the problem was the different shifts he and his wife worked, but they thought there was little they could do about that. That problem was compounded by the difficulties they had getting away for their Saturdays together.

As we addressed those difficulties, it didn't seem that any of them were major obstacles that could not be addressed by better planning, such as giving attention to many of these things when they first developed rather than waiting. Pastor J agreed to work on not letting things pile up until the weekend, and one of his projects before our next session was to talk to his wife about ways they could ensure an early Saturday departure for their time together.

However, Pastor J wanted more than just Saturdays with his wife. As we explored the options, he identified one he thought the church leaders might agree to. He would talk to them about allowing him to take two fifth Sundays a year off in addition to his regular vacation. Even though it was only two days a year, it was something to look forward to and would provide them with two more long weekends they could spend together.

Session Two

Pastor J had both good news and bad news to report at the start of our session. He and his wife agreed to work harder to make sure nothing—especially procrastination—would keep them from their Saturday getaways, but the church leadership had rejected his request for two additional Sundays off a year. This was frustrating to Pastor J, and made him feel like they did not care about him or his family. Pastor J's discouragement led to his desire to spend our second session talking about burnout.

I asked him some questions about how this pastorate compared to the others he had. He had nothing but good things to say about his previous pastorates and little good to say about this one. It became obvious that his problems with this church went beyond their refusal to give him two additional Sundays off. He regretted leaving his previous church for this one, even though at the time he felt he was following God's leading to attend seminary. He had never felt fulfilled as a pastor in his church. Many of the things he identified as important to him appeared not to be important to his church. His assignment before our next session was to develop a personal mission and purpose statement and send it to me for review.

Session Three

I received Pastor J's personal mission statement by email a couple of weeks after our previous session. Although he thought it was rough, I found it to be thorough and thought it reflected a lot of honest soul searching on his part. Much of it centered around his continued growth as an individual and a minister and being able to lead a church in intentional ministry to its community. His statement also contained a significant commitment to his family's well-being. As we discussed his mission statement during our third session, we both sensed that his ministry at his present church might be nearing its end because he thought the statement was completely at odds with anything the church was interested in.

This session was somewhat painful as Pastor J contemplated the need to leave his church. Even with his frustrations with the congregation, and especially the leadership, it was obvious he had strong feelings for them. In some ways, leaving felt like admitting he had failed. On the other hand, it did not seem that his gifts and passion for ministry were a good fit for this congregation. Pastor J had much to consider before our next session.

Session Four

As I expected, Pastor J announced at the start of our session that he had decided his ministry at his present church was complete. As he compared his personal mission statement with what the church wanted in a pastor, he decided he was not a good fit. He was ready to resign and seek a new place of employment, but there were a couple of things he wanted to complete before announcing his resignation. For some time, he had been involved in trying to reduce the number of committees in the church, and he wanted to complete that task before moving on. He also wanted to ensure that they completed the budget for the next church year.

When I asked Pastor J who could help him in his desire to move, I was surprised when he said no one. His church was a member of a fairly large, active judicatory of a denomination different from mine. In my current ministry role, I am expected to assist churches in their searches for new pastors as well as pastors who want to move to another church. Pastor J explained that he would receive no assistance from his denominational and judicatory leadership, which is why I have called Pastor J the abandoned pastor. Even though he was active in his association's bivocational pastor's group, he felt alone as he contemplated a huge transition. He said the leader of his judicatory would not know him if he walked into the leader's office. I asked if any of the churches or pastors received assistance when they were making a leadership change, and he replied that only the larger churches received such help.

I do not know if Pastor J's claims are true, but I do know his denomination well enough to know that their churches and pastors do not receive as much assistance in pastoral transitions as what my denomination offers our churches and pastors. Regardless, his perception was that, during one of the most stressful times in a pastor's life, he was alone as he sought a new place to serve.

I have worked with and coached enough bivocational ministers to know that Pastor J's perception is not uncommon. Many of them feel abandoned by denominational leaders and even other pastors. They feel they have no one who understands them and their concerns, and they are left to fight their battles alone. I explained to Pastor J that I would be glad to assist him as much as I could with his search. At that point, he began asking questions about the denomination I serve and some general topics on the search process. For the remainder of this session, I served more as a mentor to Pastor J than a coach.

Session Five

We began our fifth session with Pastor J explaining the work he had done on the church's budget and financial reports. He was still pushing for a reduction in the number of committees in the church but wasn't getting a lot of support from the congregation. Since our last session he had updated his profile and sent it to a few friends in ministry to see if they knew of possible churches he could serve.

Part of this session was similar to the previous one. At times, I acted as a coach, and at other times I mentored. One of my coaching questions was what Pastor J was looking for in a church. He had some general ideas, but it was obvious he had not thought it through. We began to discuss some questions he might consider asking a pastor search committee to help him better understand the church and get a sense of whether it might be a good match for his gifts and passions. I referred him to one of my books, *The Bivocational Pastor: Two Jobs, One Ministry*, so he could see some of the questions I had asked search committees, but I cautioned him that he should use that list only to help him compile his own list. His assignment before our next session was to write out a list of possible questions.

Session Six

Pastor J began our final session by sharing his decision that he would not announce his resignation until after the first of the new year. He did not want to distract from the holidays, and he thought he would need that much time to complete the projects he had been working on. He had prepared a list of questions to ask search committees, which we reviewed. I affirmed that his questions looked like a good way to help him identify the right church to match his personal mission and purpose.

We concluded our time by talking about the changes that had occurred in his life since our coaching relationship had begun. He felt more at peace with himself and with ministry because he knew what he had to do to enjoy ministry again. At his request I sent Pastor J's résumé out to a few churches in our denomination that I knew were looking for a bivocational minister.

Debrief

There is an interesting postscript to my relationship with Pastor J. Unlike many of the pastors I've coached, Pastor J and I had once met at a bivocational pastor's conference before we began our coaching relationship. A few months after the coaching sessions ended, I ran into Pastor J at a rest stop in West Virginia, where I had stopped on a trip to get gas and some lunch. He told me he had been meeting with a pastor search committee in another state. A few weeks later,

I received an email from Pastor J sharing that the church had called him to be their pastor. Although we have not resumed a formal coaching relationship, I do get an occasional email from him with some specific questions about ministry. I do not know how much support he receives from his current judicatory leaders, but I do know Pastor J does not feel abandoned anymore.

My ability to assist Pastor J was limited since I was not a member of his denomination and had no influence with the churches. I could, and did, send his résumé to a few churches in my denomination, but he really wanted to remain in the only denomination he had always served. What I *could* do to assist him was assure him that he was not alone. I could offer encouragement, support, and affirmation. Affirmation is pure gold to many bivocational ministers, especially the ones who feel alone in their ministries.

Pastor J has emailed since beginning his position at his new church. He has had some challenges there but nothing he could not handle, and he is much more comfortable serving there. It appears to be a better match for his gifts and mission.

THE CAVEAT

In this final section of the book I want to speak to the denominational and judicatory leaders who are reading this book. I recently spent a week leading seminars for bivocational ministers in a judicatory. One of the judicatory leaders who attended each seminar had recently been given ministering to bivocational ministers as one of his assignments. He told me that it had been years since he had been a bivocational minister and really didn't remember a lot about that experience. He had purchased a couple of my books to learn more about bivocational ministry, and that was why I had been invited to lead the seminars.

Chances are you are experiencing an increase in bivocational ministers within your tribe, and you may realize like my friend that you really don't know much about bivocational ministry or the issues those ministers face in the 21st century. You want to support them in their work but aren't sure how to best do that. This section is written especially for you.

CHAPTER THIRTEEN

A WORD TO DENOMINATIONAL AND JUDICATORY LEADERS

In the late 1970s I felt called by God to enter the ministry. My church agreed to license me, and I contacted our judicatory leader to make myself available for pulpit supply, revivals, or to serve a small church as a pastor. In a few weeks I received his reply. He told me to complete my seminary education and then contact him; he would be glad to help me find a place to serve once I had my master's degree. That presented a problem. I was married with two children. I had a good job that paid an above-average salary. We had debt. And I didn't have a bachelor's degree.

My judicatory leader had basically just asked me to place my whole life on hold for the next seven years to earn a degree before he would begin to assist me in living out what God had called me to do. I did not do that. Instead, I found a small church in a different denomination, located in our community, and spent the next twenty years serving that congregation.

After a couple of years as pastor I decided to pursue some theological education, so I enrolled in a Bible school located an hour from my house. I added that to my other job and my pastorate, but I felt strongly that the education I would receive from that school would benefit my ministry. One semester some people from the denomination came to my class to ask if any of us would consider doing some church planting in an adjacent state. I asked if they would accept bivocational people as church planters. He quickly said church planting was no work for a bivocational person; church planters had to be completely dedicated to their ministry and not distracted by another job.

The mindset in those days was that bivocational ministry was limited to persons who were not serious about doing ministry, people who could not handle a "real" church, and fly-by-night preachers looking to pick up some extra money. There were few resources available for bivocational ministers, and many judicatory and denominational leaders had little interest in those ministers and the churches they served. Their focus was on the larger churches, and most denominational programming and support went to those churches.

Despite the neglect small churches with bivocational pastors often experienced in those days, they did not close their doors. Even more surprising, God did not stop calling individuals to bivocational ministry, and those persons who were called did not refuse just because they knew they would receive little support. The good news is, I am meeting more and more denominational leaders who understand the value bivocational ministers can bring to their churches and to the denomination.

But sometimes leaders aren't sure how they can best help the bivocational ministers who serve in their districts, regions, or conventions. Perhaps this is where you find yourself. Maybe you've tried to schedule some training events but found it's hard to count on bivocational ministers to attend. They are often frustrating to work with because they don't always play by denominational expectations. They color outside the lines and, frankly, don't seem to care if that bothers people.

Perhaps it's time to consider coaching. Much of the coaching I've done has been over the phone, so it wasn't necessary to arrange a time to meet, which was helpful because, for many bivocational ministers, there really are no convenient times to meet that don't take them away from something else. Because coaching always works from the agenda of the person being coached, you can be certain you are always focusing your conversation on the most important issues the minister is facing. One of the reasons bivocational ministers often don't attend training events is that these events do not address the specific issues bivocational ministers face. With coaching you are always dealing with the most pressing issue the minister has in his or her life.

Coaching also doesn't require you to be an expert on every issue. The best coaches spend their time asking questions rather than giving answers or advice. By asking powerful questions, the coach is often able to pull out of the coaching client the best answers to the problem. The person being coached often already knows what needs to be done but just needs to have someone help him or her surface that answer and give affirmation.

Before you can successfully coach someone, you need a couple of things. You need at least an introductory understanding of coaching and some coaching techniques you can use. There are a number of good resources available to help you that can be found with minimal research. You also need to be clear on some specific things about bivocational ministers. If you are a denominational or judicatory leader who isn't sure about the validity of bivocational ministry, I hope this will help you better understand those individuals and the churches they serve so you can become supportive. It is impossible to make a blanket statement about bivocational ministers and include everyone, but hopefully I can help you can get a general grasp of what is needed.

Bivocational Ministers Feel Called to Bivocational Ministry

Bivocational ministers do not have to do what they do. Most of them have other jobs that provide sufficient support for themselves and their families. Most are not looking to the ministry for supplemental income, having decided that pastoring a church would be easier than getting a part-time job at a convenience store. When I began my pastoral ministry, my tithe check was often almost as much as my paycheck from the church. I didn't pastor that church for additional income; I was there because I was certain God had called me there. Most bivocational ministers are in their places of ministry for the same reason.

Some people question whether the call to bivocational ministry is valid. I have read church leaders who said that another job is an interference to ministry and that persons with a second job have not been called to ministry. I have responded to some of those people by pointing out Paul's tentmaking career, but they usually respond that, while that may have been acceptable then, since the church was just getting started, it is not a valid ministry option today, which is not a claim that can be backed by Scripture.

Bivocational ministers want to serve the kingdom of God and are willing to do that by serving usually smaller churches. These are churches that are often shunned by fully-funded pastors. Without bivocational ministers who can financially support themselves and their families with outside income, these churches likely could not remain open, and any ministry they provide would be lost.

There are those who would argue that perhaps these churches *should* close their doors, and bivocational ministry just allows churches that have long lost any value to the kingdom to remain open. In some cases that might be true, but that argument has been addressed elsewhere. We should be very careful, however, when saying that any church has lost its value to the kingdom of God. God works on his own time, and it is not our place to decide whether a church is making a valid contribution to the kingdom (barring, of course, extreme circumstances).

Most bivocational ministers feel called to do what they do. They knew it would be a challenge to add ministry to their other responsibilities, but they also knew they would be disobeying God if they didn't. What they want most from their denominational and judicatory leaders is affirmation of that call.

Bivocational Ministers Feel Isolated

Unfortunately, many bivocational ministers do not believe their call is affirmed and respected. One of the most common complaints I hear from bivocational ministers is that they get no assistance from their denominational leaders, a perception that comes from a number of experiences they have in ministry.

It is easier for a judicatory leader to call on a fully-funded pastor than it is to contact a bivocational minister. We can meet fully-funded pastors for breakfast or lunch or schedule visits to their church offices as we pass through their communities. However, bivocational ministers often have to be at their second jobs during pastoral visits. To spend time with bivocational ministers often means we have to do so in the evening, and that means both judicatory leaders and bivocational ministers will have to take away precious time from their families. It's not easy to schedule a time to meet with bivocational ministers, so denominational leaders often don't bother. Months may pass by without the bivocational minister receiving any personal contact from someone from the denominational or judicatory office.

Training events or other denominational gatherings are often held during the week when bivocational ministers are unable to attend. The message bivocational ministers receive when they are invited to the next training event or pastoral gathering on a Tuesday morning is that their presence is not really expected or even desired. Unfortunately, even scheduling events on Saturday will not guarantee that bivocational ministers can attend. Saturday is often a day they need to finish up sermon preparation or make some church visits or do something with their families. Unless an event's topic really appeals to them or they know the event was developed specifically for them, they more often than not will choose to do something else that day.

The issue of ordination can also cause bivocational ministers to feel isolated. When denominations put various educational requirements on ordination, they can cause some of their ministers to feel like second-class citizens. The denomination I serve requires a master of divinity degree for ordination. Our polity does allow an individual church to ordain someone who does not have that degree, but the ordination is considered less than a fully recognized one, creating an unnecessary division of hierarchy between ministers. To further compound the problem, all of us in denominational work have known a few pastors who did meet all the educational requirements and were fully ordained yet left a trail of broken churches behind them. No degree can take the place of being called by God to serve as a minister, and no degree guarantees that a person will be successful in ministry.

I do not have the master of divinity degree. I went to my church with no education beyond high school. While serving that church, I graduated from a Bible school then enrolled in a secular university to earn my bachelor's degree. Only in recent years did I earn a master of arts in religion and a doctor of ministry degree. I still lack the master of divinity degree our denomination requires, and my ordination is a local ordination I received from Hebron Baptist Church in 1982.

Another way bivocational ministers can feel isolated is when they look at the people who are often called to be up front at various events. When was the last time your denomination or judicatory had a bivocational minister as the keynote speaker at one of your major events? How often are bivocational ministers and/or their churches highlighted in your publications? Do you ever intentionally seek bivo-cationally pastored churches as locations for events in your district? Doing any of these things will send a strong message to bivocational ministers that they are an important part of your organization.

When I began my pastorate, I introduced myself to the other pas-tors in our association, each of whom was fully funded. They predict-ed I would not survive six months in the church I had just started serving. As a brand-new pastor, that prediction from my own fellow colleagues was hardly encouraging, which meant I had no one to talk to. Too many bivocational pastors run into similar challenges and end up leaving ministry prematurely. Having a coach walk with them during that first year or two of ministry could help prevent some of the problems they encounter or help them find solutions for the ones they do experience. Not many bivocationally pastored churches have the resources or the understanding to offer a coaching relationship as part of the benefit package, nor do most of them pay enough for bivocational ministers to afford to seek coaching on their own, which is why it becomes important for judicatory leaders themselves to con-sider offering such relationships to new pastors in their districts.

Bivocational Ministers Want Relevant Training

As mentioned previously, a common frustration experienced by many in denominational and judicatory leadership is the absence of bivocational ministers at most of the training events they offer. Even those offered on the weekends suffer from the lack of bivocational ministers' attendance, making it easy to draw the incorrect and unfair conclusion that bivocational ministers are not interested in training. Most bivocational ministers simply find it too difficult to fit it into their already too busy schedules.

The training they seek falls into two categories. Some would like to pursue formal education but are not sure how they can. When I first enrolled in Bible school I sought practical training that would enable me to serve my church better, but the years I spent there made me fall in love with learning, and I found that the more I learned, the better minister I became. Because of my full-time job and my pastorate, I could only go to school part time. It took me four years to complete the two-year program, but I enjoyed the learning experience so much that I soon enrolled in a nearby university to work on my bachelor's degree, which took another seven years. A few years ago I decided to return to school and earn a master's degree then made the decision to pursue a doctorate.

Every step of the way, people challenged my decisions. When I enrolled for the bachelor's degree and told people I expected it to take me seven years, they asked, "How old will you be in seven years?" I explained that, school or no school, I would be forty-six years old in seven years, and I decided that I preferred to be forty-six with a bachelor's degree. Years later they asked the same question when enrolled in the doctoral program. I anticipated graduating when I was sixty-one, which I did, but it was never about obtaining degrees; it was about the education. I went to school to gain knowledge and wisdom and to grow as a person.

Our judicatory has a school (the Church Leadership Institute) where we train lay leaders and bivocational ministers. Occasionally, some of our graduates want more after they complete our program, and they go on to enroll in universities or seminaries. It's exciting to see bivocational ministers who want to continue their formal education.

Other bivocational ministers want specialized, seminar-type training to help them in areas in which they feel weak. Some want to learn how to prepare and deliver better sermons. Others want instruction on administrative issues. One of the driving factors that caused me to seek enrollment in the Bible college was my weakness in pastoral care and counseling. While in the pastorate, I also attended a three-day workshop on conflict management and resolution that I found helpful. Many bivocational pastors would benefit from such training and would attend if the training were offered at times that fit their schedules.

Unfortunately, there is that time constraint again. Our Church Leadership Institute offers classes on Saturdays at a centrally located college in Indiana. Each course consists of four class sessions held over a two-month period. Students can take up to four courses a year and can complete the basic program in as little as two years. The diploma program takes an additional year of classes. The Church Leadership Institute has proven to be an excellent training opportunity for some of our bivocational pastors and lay leaders throughout our region, but there are many more who would benefit from it if they could only fit it into their schedules. Many bivocational ministers are understandably reluctant to commit to attending classes sixteen Saturdays a year for two or three years.

Recently, we made a change in the program that allows a person to take just one class rather than signing up for the entire program. We believe there will be several people who will want to take just one or two of the classes we offer to improve their ministry skills, and our hope is that, once they experience the benefits of taking those classes, they will want to continue their studies.

We also have to accept the fact that some of our bivocational ministers will never enroll in the Church Leadership Institute or in any other formal educational system, but that doesn't mean they do not want training and education. It is simply a time issue for them. Again, this presents a coaching opportunity for judicatory and denominational leaders. As coaches, we can walk with them through conflict situations in their churches and help them identify ways they can help promote healing. We can coach them through pastoral care issues that they may feel inadequate to address.

One of the bivocational ministers I coached (Pastor A) had a member of his congregation who had a family member dealing with a potentially serious medical condition. He was concerned about how to minister to the family, especially since the person with the illness seldom attended church. During one coaching call, I was able to help him identify some resources in his community that could help him better minister to the individual and her family. This pastor lived several states away. I knew nothing of the area or what resources might exist, but as the coach, I didn't need that information. He had that information but had not yet accessed it. It didn't take more than two or three coaching questions for him to realize that he had numerous resources at his disposal, and this knowledge removed a lot of his anxiety.

Coaching will not replace education, but it can be a tool judicatory leaders use to help bivocational ministers deal with their ministry weaknesses. Continue to provide meaningful, practical training opportunities for your bivocational ministers, but supplement those opportunities with coaching to impact the greatest number of your bivocational ministers.

After serving for the past twelve years in judicatory ministry, I have concluded that intentionally entering into a coaching relationship with the new pastors who come into my area is a more effective use of my time than some of the other things I've tried. It may be time to set aside some of the things we've historically done as judicatory leaders, and begin to focus on things that will help lead to healthier leaders and healthier churches. It is possible that providing a coaching relationship for new pastors who come to your churches will have the greatest long-term impact of anything else you will do.

Judicatories and judicatory leaders could also offer to provide a coaching relationship to every *new* bivocational minister. Such a relationship might last for at least one year to help get pastors established in their ministries and to help them address potential issues they will experience. The judicatory I serve now provides six to twelve months of coaching for all new pastors. Coaching is available for both bivocational and fully-funded pastors, whether they are first-time ministers or just new to our judicatory. We do not require that they accept the coaching we offer, but most of them have agreed to be coached. Although it is too early to know if this will produce the results we hope for, the new pastors I have coached have reported that it has been helpful to them.

Finally, I recently spent a day training church leaders in one denomination that is preparing to offer coaching to its bivocational ministers. They recognized the potential benefits of providing such coaching and asked me to train those who had agreed to serve as coaches. I believe this will be a growing trend in many denominations, and I encourage any denomination or judicatory with bivocational ministers to consider providing such a service.

If there is a lack of knowledge or ability regarding coaching, I highly recommend you look into receiving training in coaching techniques. In 2012, I led a training for a group of pastors who agreed to be coaches to bivocational ministers in their district. I am willing to lead similar trainings for other judicatories and denominations, and there are certainly other coaches who can do the same thing. This can be a great way to develop people who can coach your bivocational ministers, or—of course—to develop your own coaching skills.

Bivocational Ministers Want to Live Balanced Lives

A desire to live a balanced life may sound like a contradiction to an outsider to bivocational ministry. Someone might argue, *If they want to live balanced lives, perhaps they shouldn't be bivocational ministers!* However, remember that bivocational ministers feel called to serve the kingdom through ministry, and many feel specifically called to bivocational ministry. A desire to serve bivocationally does not mean they *want* to sacrifice their own well-being or that of their families. Unfortunately, that does happen sometimes when bivocational pastors neglect to practice good self-care or take time for their families, but I've never met a bivocational minister who intentionally set out to ruin his or her own health or damage his or her relationships with family members.

Virtually every bivocational minister I have coached has mentioned the challenges he or she faces with time issues. Most of them feel overwhelmed. In some cases, it has already caused considerable strain in their families and/or has impacted their health. In some cases, they just need someone to give them permission to back off a little.

They need a coach who will help them identify areas in their lives and ministries they can change that would free up some time.

Most bivocational ministers try to do too much, and one of the reasons for this is that their churches try to compete with large churches in the number of ministries and programs they offer. In several of my seminars, I tell small-church leaders that their churches will accomplish more by doing less. They would be more effective in their ministries by focusing on one or two things they can do well and letting other things go.

For instance, every church does *not* have to have a youth program, especially if there are only two teenagers in the church and no one feels called to lead such a program. I know that rubs some small churches the wrong way because they believe the youth are the future of the church, but if there are only two of them, then that church doesn't have much of a future, does it? Once churches can get beyond that mindset, they will find there are a number of ministries they can offer that will provide the church with a good future and make a better impact on people's lives *now*.

Churches that offer too many programs they are not equipped to do with excellence often expect the pastor to keep each of them running, which does nothing but wear out the pastor. There is a limit to the number of plates a person can keep spinning, regardless of how committed to ministry he or she might be. If you go beyond that limit, some of those plates will come crashing to the ground, and the ensuing impact will not be helpful to the church or its pastoral leadership.

Pastors also need someone who can coach their congregations. Many pastors find it difficult to advocate for themselves to the leaders of their churches. In our denomination, many churches expect the pastor to leave the business meeting when next year's budget is being discussed since it includes the pastor's salary and benefit package.

Pastors are not expected to ask for salary increases or improvements to their benefit packages, and some churches might force their pastors to resign if they dared to request an increase. Many of the pastors I've met are also reluctant to talk with their congregational leaders about the need for more vacation time (or *any* vacation, for that matter), time away from the church, or help in some area of church work. Pastors are reluctant to suggest that churches eliminate programming, even if said programs have not been effective for years. They need someone who can come in, challenge the church's thinking about some of these things, and coach them toward new ways of thinking and behaving. Some churches call bivocational ministers and pay bivocational salaries but expect the services of fully-funded pastors. Unless someone challenges that thinking, pastors are likely to burn out trying to meet those expectations and do serious harm to themselves and other family members.

Every time the opportunity presents itself, I encourage churches to consider the benefits of giving their pastors time off. Most bivocationally pastored churches I know give their pastors two weeks of vacation. I challenge them to increase that to four weeks. I remind them that time off is the cheapest thing they can give their pastors. The only additional expense is the honorarium the church will pay someone to fill the pulpit those additional Sundays, and if that is overwhelming, a layperson in the church can always preach. Why not seize an opportunity to empower laypeople? An extra couple of weeks will be less costly to the church than the cost of seeking a new pastor when the one they have finally resigns due to exhaustion or health issues.

I am convinced one reason some pastors resign from their churches is simply to have a few weeks to relax. It is not uncommon in our region for it to take eighteen to twenty-four months to find a new pastor, especially if the church seeks a bivocational one. Even if it only takes three to four months, it is costly—financially and in other ways—to search for a new pastor. The church loses whatever momentum it may have had with the previous pastor. The new pastor will need time to know people, to know the church, and to seek God's vision for the church. It will take years for new pastors to earn the trust of their congregations before they will be able to provide leadership, and the smaller the church and the more frequent the pastoral turnover has been, the longer it will take.

I challenge churches to consider the effectiveness of their current ministries and how well those ministries represent the current giftedness of the membership, their passion for ministry, and the needs of their community. Just because a ministry was productive ten years ago does not mean it continues to be effective today. People move in and out of communities, and their needs change. Even in smaller, rural communities where people think they know everyone, chances are they don't. There are new people there who may have different needs from those who have lived there for a long time. To impact their lives for Jesus Christ, the church must be able to address those needs. Unfortunately, in many smaller churches, they cannot even think about doing so because their people, including the pastor, are too busy doing things that make little, if any, difference in people's lives today. Many bivocational pastors know this but find it difficult to talk to the church about it because these unfruitful activities are often someone's sacred cows. They need judicatory and denominational leadership to be able to coach congregations to help them see that their ministries need to change if they want to continue to reach people for Christ.

Bivocational Ministers Are an Asset to Your Churches

Virtually every denominational leader with whom I've spoken in recent years tells me that the number of bivocational ministers in their denominations is growing, and they expect that will continue for the foreseeable future. While many of them might prefer for their churches to grow to the point that they could continue to employ fully-funded pastors, that is not the reality.

The good news is that many bivocational ministers are doing a great job serving their churches. They have proven to be an asset to churches and to denominations, and more than a few have helped turn around struggling churches and take them to a place where they are able to offer effective ministry to their members and communities. They deserve our support, and with that support, they will become even more effective in their service.

Support can come from many avenues. It comes through encouragement, taking time to be with them, taking their schedules into account when scheduling events, publicly recognizing the important roles they play in their churches and in the life of their denominations, and providing them with the resources they and their churches need. Not surprisingly by this point in the book, coaching can cover each of these avenues.

Promoting the fact that coaching is available for bivocational ministers in your judicatory provides public affirmation of the importance of bivocational ministry, and coaching can provide some of the resources your bivocational ministers need for their personal and ministerial growth. Coaching is an effective way of supporting and resourcing your ministry leaders. Your churches and denomination can only benefit when you begin to coach your bivocational ministers.

AFTERWORD

In 2000 I began an organization called Bivocational Ministries to provide bivocational ministers and small-church leaders with resources that can help them both personally and in their ministries. In addition to the books I've written, Bivocational Ministries offers a number of other resources that we encourage you to consider.

- The Bivocational Ministries website (*bivocationalministries .com*) analyzes different challenges faced by bivocational ministers and offers practical help, encouragement, and various resources to assist them.

- I write a blog dedicated to bivocational ministry (*bivocational ministry.blogspot.com*) that offers a community for ministers to read my views on various topics and the opportunity for others to respond. The blog works best when it creates a dialogue from which we can learn from one another.

- I invite you to find and friend-request me on Facebook (*facebook .com/dennis.bickers*). Facebook gives me an opportunity to let people know my speaking schedule and provide various updates on what is happening in the world of bivocational ministry.

- Follow me on Twitter @DennisBickers. There I direct people to various resources, either my own or ones I've found that I believe will be helpful or interesting.

I offer coaching to bivocational ministers and denominational leaders. If you believe a coach could help you move forward with your ministry and/or life, please feel free to contact me via one of the various media mentioned. I also have a number of workshops developed for small-church leaders that I have been privileged to lead for various denominations in the U.S. and Canada. A list of these workshops can be found on my website and blog. Denominational leaders should contact me if they find any of them might be helpful to the small-church leaders in their districts.

Lastly, I have published a number of other books with Beacon Hill Press, and each of them provides helpful information to anyone—pastor or lay leader—who serves bivocationally or in a small-church setting. These include:

- *The Bivocational Pastor: Two Jobs, One Ministry*
- *The Healthy Small Church: Diagnosis and Treatment for the Big Issues*
- *Intentional Ministry in a Not-So-Mega Church: Becoming a Missional Community*
- *The Healthy Pastor: Easing the Stresses of Ministry*
- *The Healthy Community: Moving Your Church Beyond Tunnel Vision*

NOTES

Introduction

1. Gary R. Collins, *Christian Coaching: Helping Others Turn Potential Into Reality* (Colorado Springs, CO: NavPress, 2001), 16.

Chapter 1

1. Connie Davis Bushey and William Perkins, "Bivocational ministers ask NAMB for office to support their work," *Baptist Press*, June 7, 2006, *http://www .baptistpress.org/bpnews.asp?id=23417* (accessed August 21, 2006).

2. Archibald D. Hart, *Coping with Depression in the Ministry and Other Helping Professions* (Dallas: Word Publishing, 1984), 18.

3. Leonard Sweet, *Carpe Mañana* (Grand Rapids: Zondervan, 2001), 93.

4. Dennis W. Bickers, *The Tentmaking Pastor: The Joy of Bivocational Ministry* (Grand Rapids: Baker Books, 2000), 75- 86.

5. Dennis Bickers, *The Healthy Pastor: Easing the Stresses of Ministry* (Kansas City: Beacon Hill Press, 2010), 11- 20.

6. Patricia Change, "The Clergy Job Market: What are the opportunities for ministry in the 21st century?" Hartford Institute for Religion Research, *http://hirr .hartsem.edu/leadership/clergyresources_clergyjobs.html* (accessed December 3, 2008).

7. Lawrence W. Farris, *Dynamics of Small Town Ministry* (Herndon, VA: The Alban Institute, 2000), 2.

Chapter 2

1. Collins, 15.

2. Daniel Harkavy, *Becoming a Coaching Leader: The Proven Strategies for Building a Team of Champions* (Nashville: Thomas Nelson, 2007), 36.

3. Tony Stoltzfus, *Leadership Coaching: The Disciplines, Skills, and Heart of a Christian Coach* (Charleston, SC: BookSurge Publishing, 2005), 65.

4. Stoltzfus, 40.

5. John Whitmore, *Coaching for Performance: GROWing People, Performance, and Purpose*, 3rd ed. (London: Nicholas Brealey Publishing, 2002), 8.

6. Jane Creswell, *Christ-Centered Coaching: 7 Benefits for Ministry Leaders* (St. Louis: Lake Hickory Resources, 2006), 14.

7. Linda J. Miller and Chad W. Hall, *Coaching for Christian Leaders: A Practical Guide* (St. Louis: Chalice Press, 2007), 94.

Chapter 4

1. John C. Maxwell, *Failing Forward* (Nashville: Thomas Nelson, 2000).

2. George W. Bullard, Jr. *Pursuing the Full Kingdom Potential of Your Congregation* (St. Louis: Lake Hickory Resources, 2005), 205.

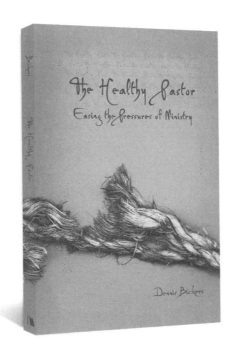

The Healthy Pastor seeks to provide insights into the expectations churches and ministers have of the pastor's role. Dennis Bickers addresses some of the common pressure points every minister experiences and provides solutions to those pressures. Ministers will be challenged to create balance in several areas of their lives: their relationship with God, family, the church, their self, and—for bivocational ministers—their second job.

The Healthy Pastor
Easing the Pressures of Ministry
Dennis Bickers
ISBN 978-0-8341-2553-7

BEACON HILL PRESS
OF KANSAS CITY

www.beaconhillbooks.com
Available online or wherever books are sold.